Irasshai: Welcome to Japanese Workbook, Volume 2

An Interactive, Multimedia Course in Beginning Japanese

Cliff Walker and Ellen Jones-Walker
K. Negrelli, K. Suzuki and S. Suzuki

Irasshai is produced and operated by Georgia Public Broadcasting.

Published by Booksurge Publishing, 7290-B Investment Dr., Charleston, SC 29418.

First edition, 1997, by Cliff Walker and Ellen Jones-Walker.

Printed in the U.S.A.

ISBN: 1-4196-8560-0
Library of Congress Card No. 9781419685606

INTRODUCTION

Contents and Organization of the Workbook

This workbook, a companion to the textbook, *Irasshai*: Welcome to Japanese, Volume 2, is designed to provide additional practices that will assist in your development of a beginning level of proficiency in listening, speaking, reading and writing Japanese, as well as your understanding of Japanese culture. It is recommended for use in conjunction with the textbook, 65 interactive video lessons, and website, which offers ancillary reading and writing support.

The workbook contains four sections:

Assignments - corresponding to the lessons in the textbook, they are divided into two parts, based on a pace of one lesson every two days. It is suggested that each part of the assignments be completed each day following the video lesson and interactive activities. While there is a variety of assignments, such as memorizing vocabulary, reviewing the notes of the lessons, and preparing for interactive activities, emphasis is placed on assignments involving reading and writing Japanese. A total of 70 *kanji* are taught in Lessons 7 ~ 60.

Optional Writing Practices - *kanji* in the textbook are divided into those introduced for reading recognition only and those introduced for both writing as well as reading. For those students who are interested in the additional challenge of learning to write all *kanji*, these optional writing practices will be useful.

Particle Practices - these practices reiterate the explanations and example sentences found in the textbook. They provide periodic review of the usage of particles and offer further opportunities to demonstrate command of Japanese grammar.

Reading and Writing Practices - these supplementary practices complement the assignments and particle practices. They allow for reinforcement of basic vocabulary and grammatical patterns and enable you to gradually progress towards more personalized, creative writing tasks.

Both Particle Practices and Reading and Writing Practices span a number of lessons. The lessons covered by these practices are included on each individual assignment and will indicate at what point you will be able to complete them.

Answer keys to the Assignments, Particle Practices, and Reading and Writing Practices can be found in the Teachers' Guide to *Irasshai:* Welcome to Japanese.

Workbook-Specific Conventions

A number of assignments in this workbook require you to complete writing tasks and then review your work. The following editing symbols are tools to assist you and to help develop a uniform pattern when checking.

EDITING SYMBOLS

∧	a word is missing	X (above word)	omit word
∧∧	two words are missing	___ (under word)	change word or part of word
▲	*hiragana/katakana* is missing	← / → (above word)	move word in direction of
⇩	the *kana* below the arrow is not		arrow to a different position
	formed correctly		in the sentence

EXAMPLE: たなかさん　たんじょびで　と　ともだち　すレをにたべまして。

(Tanaka-san　tanjobi-de　to　tomodachi　sushi-o ni tabemashite.)

CORRECTED: たなかさんは たんじょうびに ともだちと すしを たべました。

(Tanaka-san-wa　tanjoobi-ni　tomodachi-to sushi-o　tabemashita.)

Acknowledgements

We would like to express deep gratitude to Mr. Cliff Walker and Ms. Ellen Jones-Walker, authors of the original *Irasshai* textbook, from which the Assignments portion of this workbook were drawn. We are also grateful for the individual contributions of Ms. Tomoko Aeba, Ms. Akiko Davis, Ms. Masayo Nishioka and Ms. Yoko Takeuchi, whose input and insight have enabled the creation of this supplementary workbook. Reformatting of the original and subsequently created *Irasshai* materials has truly been a cooperative endeavor, and we would like to give special thanks to Ms. Jennifer Barclay, multimedia designer whose contemporary artwork brings fun and freshness to the *Irasshai* textbook series, Mr. Nick Bess, arranger of the cover design; Ms. Lisa Hannabach, editor extraordinaire, with her razor-sharp sense of detail and precision; and last but not least, Mr. Danny Hong, graphic designer, whose optimism, speed, technical skills and patience have miraculously pulled the many pieces of the *Irasshai* textbooks and workbooks together.

Hiragana Chart

n	wa	ra	ya	ma	ha	na	ta	sa	ka	a
ん	わ	ら	や	ま	は	な	た	さ	か	あ
n	wa	ra	ya	ma	ha	na	ta	sa	ka	a
		り		み	ひ	に	ち	し	き	い
		ri		mi	hi	ni	chi	shi	ki	i
		る	ゆ	む	ふ	ぬ	つ	す	く	う
		ru	yu	mu	fu	nu	tsu	su	ku	u
		れ		め	へ	ね	て	せ	け	え
		re		me	he	ne	te	se	ke	e
	を	ろ	よ	も	ほ	の	と	そ	こ	お
	(w)o	ro	yo	mo	ho	no	to	so	ko	o

Katakana Chart

n	wa	ra	ya	ma	ha	na	ta	sa	ka	a
ン	ワ	ラ	ヤ	マ	ハ	ナ	タ	サ	カ	ア
n	wa	ra	ya	ma	ha	na	ta	sa	ka	a
		リ		ミ	ヒ	ニ	チ	シ	キ	イ
		ri		mi	hi	ni	chi	shi	ki	i
		ル	ユ	ム	フ	ヌ	ツ	ス	ク	ウ
		ru	yu	mu	fu	nu	tsu	su	ku	u
		レ		メ	ヘ	ネ	テ	セ	ケ	エ
		re		me	he	ne	te	se	ke	e
	ヲ	ロ	ヨ	モ	ホ	ノ	ト	ソ	コ	オ
	(w)o	ro	yo	mo	ho	no	to	so	ko	o

Table of Contents

PRELIMINARY LESSON 1
Volume 1, Part 1

PART 1

1. Read all of the notes for Preliminary Lesson 1.
If you need further review, reread the notes from the appropriate lessons in Volume 1 of the *Irasshai* textbook.

2. Review the vocabulary.

PART 2

1. Review all hiragana.
Use your flash cards. You may also find it helpful to review reading activities and assignments from Volume 1 of the *Irasshai* textbook.

2. Preview the vocabulary and notes for Preliminary Lesson 2.
Previewing is still a very important part of your assignment. Looking over the material in the next lesson before viewing the video lesson will enable you to make much better progress in learning にほんご. がんばって。

PRELIMINARY LESSON 2
Volume 1, Part 2

PART 1

1. Read all of the notes for Prelimary Lesson 2.
If you need further review, reread the notes from the appropriate lessons in Volume 1 of the *Irasshai* textbook.

2. Review the vocabulary.

PART 2

1. Review all hiragana.
Use your flash cards. You may also find it helpful to review reading activities and assignments from Volume 1 of the *Irasshai* textbook.

2. Preview the vocabulary and notes for Lesson 1 of this text.

LESSON 1
Homestay 1

PART 1

1. Read all of the notes for Lesson 1.
If you need further review, reread the notes from the appropriate lessons in Volume 1 of the *Irasshai* textbook.

2. Review the vocabulary.

3. Kakimashoo!
Write the Japanese equivalents of the following English words. Use *hiragana*. Check your work by finding the answers in the box in the textbook, Lesson 1, Interactive Activities Part 2, ❶ after you have completed the assignment.

ENGLISH		HIRAGANA
1. music	1.	
2. foods	2.	
3. Japanese	3.	

	ENGLISH		HIRAGANA
4.	(school) subject	4.	
5.	English	5.	
6.	can (do) a little	6.	
7.	like, is/are pleasing	7.	
8.	don't really like	8.	
9.	fish	9.	
10.	meat	10.	
11.	vegetables	11.	
12.	movies	12.	
13.	can't really (do)	13.	
14.	math	14.	
15.	history	15.	

PART 2

1. Kotaete kudasai.

Read each of the following questions carefully. Then write a true answer about yourself. Write each answer in *kana (hiragana/katakana)*.

1. おなまえは？

2. なんねんせい ですか。

3. がっこうは どこ ですか。

4. なんさい ですか。

5. たべものは なにが いちばん すき ですか。

6. スポーツは なにが できますか。

2. Preview the vocabulary and notes for Lesson 2.

Previewing is a very important part of your assignment. Looking over the material in the next lesson before viewing the video lesson will enable you to make much better progress in learning にほんご. がんばって。

LESSON 2
Homestay 2

PART 1

1. Read all of the notes for Lesson 2.

2. Study the vocabulary.

In addition to the words listed in the たんご (Vocabulary) section of this lesson of the textbook, be sure to review the days of the month in the box in the ぶんぽうポイント (Key Grammar Points) section.

3. Kakimashoo!

Write the following in *kana (hiragana/katakana)*. Check your work by finding the answers in the よみましょう (*Yomimashoo!*) section of the textbook. Do not include hyphens in the *kana*.

1. itsu	4. kara	7. pikunikku-ni ikimasu
2. otanjoobi	5. made	8. natsu-yasumi
3. puuru	6. gatsu	9. hoomusutei

PART 2

1. Kakimashoo!

Write the following in *kana (hiragana/katakana)*. Check your work by finding the answers in this lesson of the textbook, Interactive Activities Part 2, ❷. Do not write hyphens.

1. tenisu-o shimasu	3. sakkaa-o shimasu	5. sukii-o shimasu
2. doraibu-ni ikimasu	4. bareebooru-o shimasu	6. gorufu-o shimasu

2. Preview the vocabulary and notes for Lesson 3.

LESSON 3
Homestay 3

PART 1

1. Read all of the notes for Lesson 3.

2. Study the vocabulary.

PART 2

1. Eigo-de nan-to iimasu-ka?

Write the English equivalents of the following Japanese words for community places. Check your work by finding the words in the textbook, たんご section of this lesson or in Lessons 68 and 70 of Volume 1.

ここはどこですか。えいごでなんといいますか。

くつや　　shoe store	だいがく	えき
パンや	ちゅうがっこう	カメラや
ほんや	とけいや	ゆうびんきょく
こうえん	デパート	ふくや
ホテル	にくや	しょうがっこう
としょかん	さかなや	こうこう
ぎんこう	やおや	ケーキや
ちかてつ	えいがかん	スーパー

2. Preview the vocabulary and notes for Lesson 4.

LESSON 4
Homestay 4

1. Read all of the notes for Lesson 4.

2. Study the vocabulary.

3. Kakimashoo!
Write the following in *kana* (*hiragana/katakana*). Check your work by finding the answers in the textbook, よみましょう section of this lesson.

1. petto

4. shashin

7. okaasan

10. chichi

2. inu

5. dare

8. imooto

11. katte-imasu

3. kawaii

6. neko

9. kazoku

12. go-kyoodai

PART 2

1. Watashi-no petto
Using the information about your imaginary pet in the textbook, Interactive Activities, Part 2, complete the following description of your pet. Write all of the information (except for your pet's name) in *kana*.

わたしは ペットを かっています。ペットは _____ です。
　　　　　　　　　　　　　　　　　　　　　　　　　　(kind of pet)

なまえは _____ です。 _____ です。
　　　　　(petto-no namae)　　　　　　　　　　　　　(iro)

_____ です。 _____ を たべます。
(ookii ~ chiisai)　　　　　　　(tabemono)

にほんごが _____ 。
　　　　　　(dekimasu ~ sukoshi dekimasu ~ dekimasen ~ zenzen dekimasen)

2. Preview the vocabulary and notes for Lesson 5.

LESSON 5
Homestay 5

PART 1

1. Read all of the notes for Lesson 5.

2. Study the vocabulary.

3. Wakaru? Wakarimasu-ka?
Complete this chart by writing the plain forms of the verbs in *hiragana* and the English equivalents. Practice saying the plain form equivalent of *-masu* forms and vice versa.

POLITE FORM		PLAIN FORM		ENGLISH
わかります	wakarimasu	わかる	wakaru	understand
します	shimasu		suru	
ちがいます	chigaimasu		chigau	
いきます	ikimasu		iku	
います	imasu		iru	

POLITE FORM		PLAIN FORM		ENGLISH
ききます	kikimasu		kiku	
あります	arimasu		aru	
よみます	yomimasu		yomu	
みます	mimasu		miru	
きます	kimasu		kuru	
おきます	okimasu		okiru	
かえります	kaerimasu		kaeru	
ねます	nemasu		neru	
できます	dekimasu		dekiru	
たべます	tabemasu		taberu	
うたいます	utaimasu		utau	
のみます	nomimasu		nomu	
かいます	kaimasu		kau	
なります	narimasu		naru	

PART 2

1. Kakimashoo!

Write the following in *hiragana*. Do not write hyphens in Japanese. Check your work by finding the answers in the textbook, よみましょう section of this lesson.

1. hayai

2. nemui

3. itadakimasu

4. Doo desu-ka?

5. osoi

6. ima

7. oishii

8. asa-gohan

9. mainichi

10. hayai

2. Preview the vocabulary and notes for Lesson 6.

LESSON 6
Countries and Languages

PART 1

1. Read all of the notes for Lesson 6.

2. Learn the new vocabulary.

PART 2

1. Kakimashoo!

Choose a country whose name has appeared in this lesson. Make sure you know what language is spoken in that country. Write five true sentences in Japanese (*hiragana/katakana*) about the country to give hints as to its identity. To get some ideas for your sentences, look at the two passages in this lesson of the textbook, Interactive Activities Part 2, ❷.

Write country names in English if you do not know the Japanese words or are unsure of how to write them. Provide enough information so that the name of the country can be figured out after reading your sentences.

どこの くに ですか。

1. _____
2. _____
3. _____
4. _____
5. _____

2. Preview the vocabulary and notes for Lesson 7.

LESSON 7
Locations and Cardinal Directions

PART 1

1. Read all of the notes for Lesson 7.

2. Learn the new vocabulary.

3. Prepare for an interactive activity.
Bring a copy of a world map to the next class. You will be using it for Interactive Activities Part 2, ❷.

PART 2

1. Kakimashoo!
Choose a country whose name appeared in Lesson 6. Make sure you know where the country is located and what language is spoken in that country. Write six true sentences in Japanese (*hiragana/katakana*) about the country to give hints as to its identity. To get some ideas for your sentences, look at the two passages in the textbook, Lesson 6, Interactive Activities Part 2, ❷. Be sure to include at least one sentence with a cardinal direction (*kita, higashi, minami, nishi*).

Write country names in English if you do not know the Japanese words or are unsure of how to write them. Provide enough information so that the name of the country can be figured out after reading the sentences.

INFORMATION YOU MIGHT INCLUDE	
☑ size	☑ close to another country
☑ continent where located	☑ relative location (east of ____ , etc.)
☑ language(s) spoken	☑ a country that it is not (but that might be
☑ close to *or* far from your country	guessed because of the other hints)

どこの くに ですか。

1. _____
2. _____
3. _____
4. _____
5. _____
6. _____

2. Yomimashoo!
Practice reading the following. Cover the *roomaji* side with a piece of paper and move it down one line at a time to check your accuracy. After you have finished, write the English equivalents in the right-hand column. Check your own answers by finding the words in the textbook, かんじ ノート (Kanji Notes) section of this lesson.

かなと かんじ	ローマじ	えいご
1. 月よう日	getsu-yoobi	
2. １月	ichi-gatsu	
3. ３月	san-gatsu	
4. なん月	nan-gatsu	
5. 日よう日	nichi-yoobi	
6. かよう日	ka-yoobi	
7. たんじょう日	tanjoobi	
8. １１日	juu-ichi-nichi	
9. ２３日	ni-juu-san-nichi	
10. ２日	futsuka	
11. ３日	mikka	

3. Preview the vocabulary and notes for Lesson 8.

LESSON 8
Geography

PART 1

1. Read all of the notes for Lesson 8.

2. Learn the new vocabulary.

3. Dekimasu-ka?
Can you read the following sentence? The words are in the correct order, but there are no spaces between words. Write the *roomaji* equivalent under the sentence, leaving spaces between words but affixing particles to the preceding words. What does the sentence mean in English?

日本はちいさいですけどとてもきれいなくにです。

PART 2

1. Kakimashoo!
Write the following natural features in *hiragana*. After you have finished, check your answers by finding the words in the textbook, よみましょう section of this lesson.

1. shima 　　　　　3. yama 　　　　　5. kawa

2. mizuumi 　　　　4. umi

2. Yomimashoo!
Practice reading the following. Cover the *roomaji* side with a piece of paper and move it down one line at a time to check your accuracy. After you have finished, write the English equivalents in the right-hand column.

かなとかんじ	ローマじ	えいご
1. 木よう日	moku-yoobi	
2. 本	hon	
3. 日本	Nihon, Nippon	
4. 日本ご	nihongo	
5. 人	hito	
6. 3人	san-nin	
7. アメリカ人	amerika-jin	
8. 日本人	nihon-jin	
9. おんなの人	onna-no hito	
10. 3日	mikka	
11. かよう日	ka-yoobi	
12. 月よう日	getsu-yoobi	
13. 1月	ichi-gatsu	
14. 20日	hatsuka	
15. 2日	futsuka	
16. 14日	juu-yokka	
17. なん月	nan-gatsu	
18. 日よう日	nichi-yoobi	
19. たんじょう日	tanjoobi	
20. 11日	juu-ichi-nichi	

3. Preview the vocabulary and notes for Lesson 9.

LESSON 9
Describing with Superlatives

PART 1
---

1. Read all of the notes for Lesson 9.

2. Learn the new vocabulary.

3. Yomimashoo!
Practice reading the following. Cover the *roomaji* side with a piece of paper and move it down one line at a time to check your accuracy. After you have finished, write the English equivalents in the right-hand column. The answers can be found in the textbook, かんじノート sections of Lessons 7-9.

かなと かんじ	ローマじ	えいご
1. 小さい	chiisai	
2. 日本ごの本	nihongo-no hon	
3. 2日	futsuka	
4. なん月	nan-gatsu	
5. 日本	Nihon, Nippon	
6. 小がっこう	shoogakkoo	
7. 大すき	daisuki	
8. 月よう日	getsu-yoobi	
9. 3人	san-nin	
10. たんじょう日	tanjoobi	
11. おんなの人	onna-no hito	
12. 大がく	daigaku	
13. 木よう日	moku-yoobi	
14. 日本人	nihon-jin	
15. 日よう日	nichi-yoobi	
16. 23日	ni-juu-san-nichi	
17. 大きい	ookii	

PART 2

1. Kakimashoo!

Write five sentences in *hiragana/katakana* using the same pattern which you practiced in this lesson of the textbook, Interactive Activities Part 1, ❷.

この しつもんは いちばん かんたん です。
Kono   shitsumon-wa   ichiban   kantan   desu.

トムさんの パーティーは いちばん たのしい です。
Tomu-san-no   paatii-wa   ichiban   tanoshii   desu.

1. _____

2. _____

3. _____

4. _____

5. _____

2. Preview the vocabulary and notes for Lesson 10.

LESSON 10
Telling How Long One Has Done Something

PART 1
---

1. Read all of the notes for Lesson 10.

2. Learn the new vocabulary.

3. Complete Writing Practice ❶ Study, trace and write.

PART 2
---

1. Complete the remainder of the Writing Practice.

2. Preview the vocabulary and notes for Lesson 11.

WRITING PRACTICE

❶ Study, trace and write.

GETSU, GATSU; tsuki* (month, moon)

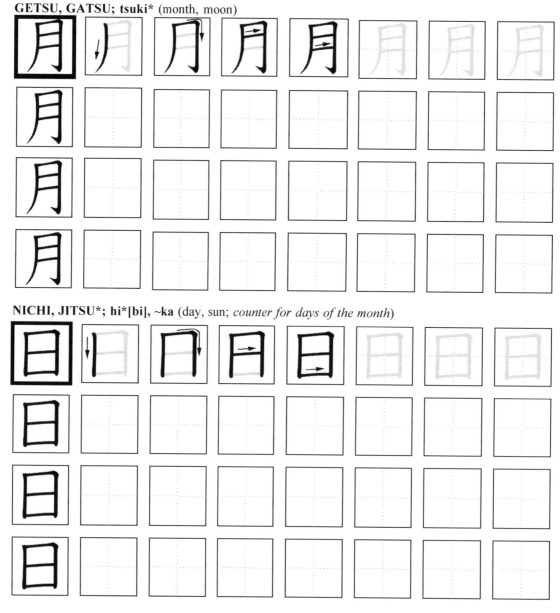

NICHI, JITSU*; hi*[bi], ~ka (day, sun; *counter for days of the month*)

❷ **Dore desu-ka?** 月　日

Below each underlined part write the corresponding *kanji*. Use the correct stroke order. Check your answers by finding the words in the かんじノート section of the textbook, Lesson 7.

1. <u>getsu</u>-yoo<u>bi</u>　　3. nan-<u>gatsu</u>　　5. tanjoo<u>bi</u>　　7. ichi-<u>gatsu</u>

2. juu-ichi-<u>nichi</u>　　4. futsu<u>ka</u>　　6. mai<u>nichi</u>　　8. <u>nichi</u>-yoo<u>bi</u>

❸ **Kakimashoo!**

Read each of the following words aloud. Then underline the part(s) which you can write in *kanji*. Rewrite the entire word, substituting the known *kanji*. Use the correct stroke order. All of these words appear in ❷.

1. いちがつ　　3. まいにち　　5. じゅういちにち　7. にちようび

2. なんがつ　　4. げつようび　　6. ふつか　　8. たんじょうび

❹ **Dekimasu-ka?**

Read each of the following sentences aloud. Underline the part(s) which you can write in *kanji* (月 and 日). Copy the entire sentence substituting the known *kanji*. The sentences appear in the textbook, かんじノート section of Lesson 7. The number of known *kanji* in each sentence is given in brackets following the sentence.

1. なんがつ でしたか。　　[1]

2. げつようび に いきました。　[2]

3. にちようび ですか。　[2]

4. みっか じゃ ない です。　[1]

❺ **More writing practice**

If you need additional practice, trace the sample *kanji* on the previous page, and then use blank writing practice sheets.

LESSON 11
Current Activities

PART 1

1. Read all of the notes for Lesson 11.

2. Complete Writing Practice ❶ Study, trace and write.

PART 2

1. Complete the remainder of the Writing Practice.

2. Preview the vocabulary and notes for Lesson 12.

❶ **Study, trace and write.**

MOKU, BOKU*; ki* [gi*] (tree, wood)

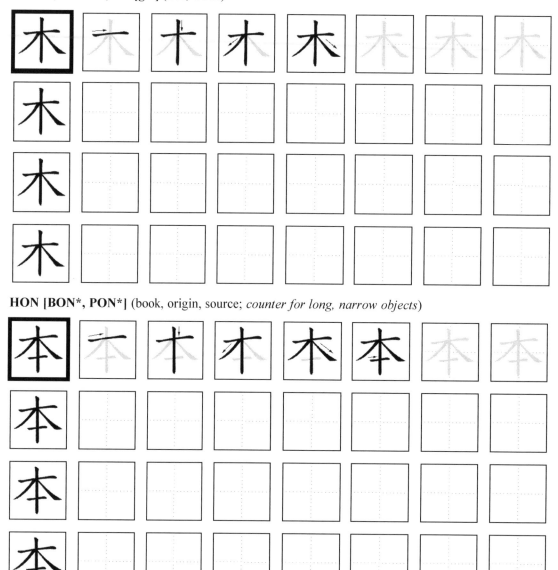

HON [BON*, PON*] (book, origin, source; *counter for long, narrow objects*)

NIN, JIN; hito, ~ri (person; *counter for people*)

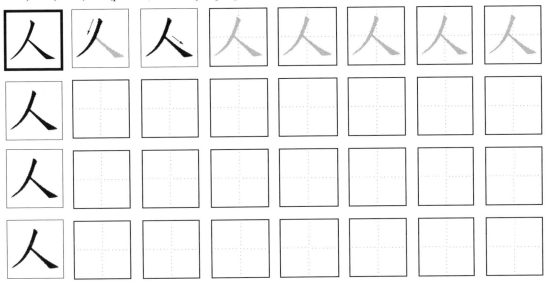

❷ **Dore desu-ka?** 月 日 木 本 人
Below each underlined part write the corresponding *kanji*. Use the correct stroke order. Check your answers by finding the words in the かんじノート sections of Lessons 7 and 8.

1. <u>moku</u>-yoo<u>bi</u>   5. juu-ichi-<u>nichi</u>   9. <u>hon</u>   13. tanjoo<u>bi</u>

2. nan-<u>gatsu</u>   6. san-<u>nin</u>   10. amerika-<u>jin</u>   14. hito<u>ri</u>

3. futa<u>ri</u>   7. ichi-<u>gatsu</u>   11. <u>getsu</u>-yoo<u>bi</u>   15. mik<u>ka</u>

4. <u>nihon-jin</u> [3 kanji]   8. <u>nichi</u>-yoo<u>bi</u>   12. futsu<u>ka</u>   16. <u>hito</u>

❸ **Kakimashoo!** 月 日 木 本 人
Read each of the following words aloud. Then underline the part(s) which you can write in *kanji*. Rewrite the entire word, substituting the known *kanji*. Use the correct stroke order. All of these words appear in ❷.

1. ひと   5. なんがつ   9. にほんじん   13. もくようび

2. ほん   6. たんじょうび   10. いちがつ   14. みっか

3. ふつか   7. ふたり   11. ひとり   15. げつようび

4. アメリカじん   8. じゅういちにち   12. にちようび   16. さんにん

❹ **Dekimasu-ka?** 月 日 木 本 人
Read each of the following sentences aloud. Underline the part(s) which you can write in *kanji*. Copy the entire sentence, substituting the known *kanji*. The number of known *kanji* in each sentence is given in brackets following the sentence. Check the textbook, かんじノート sections of Lessons 7 and 8.

1. にほんの だいがく ですか。   [2]

13

2. もくようびに しました。 [2]

3. おんなのひとが さんにん います。 [2]

4. げつようびに いきました。 [2]

❺ More writing practice
If you need additional practice, trace the sample *kanji* on the previous pages, and then use blank writing practice sheets.

LESSON 12
Talk about What Someone Was Doing

PART 1

1. Read all of the notes for Lesson 12.

2. Prepare for an interactive activity.
To be able to fully participate in this enjoyable game in Interactive Activities Part 2, ❷ read the description and procedures before class. Also review the vocabulary and sample questions and answers. In class you will want to devote as much time as you can to actually playing the game – not getting ready to play!

3. Complete Writing Practice ❶ Study, trace and write.

PART 2

1. Complete the remainder of the Writing Practice.

2. Preview the vocabulary and notes for Lesson 13.

WRITING PRACTICE
❶ Study, trace and write.

DAI, TAI*; oo(kii) (big, large, great)

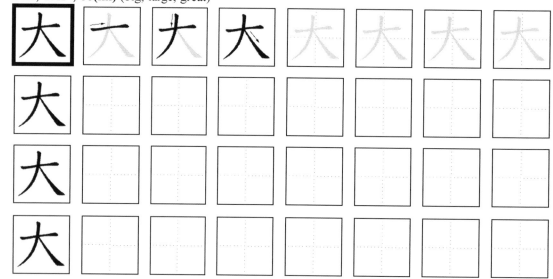

SHOO; ko*, o*, chii(sai) (small, little)

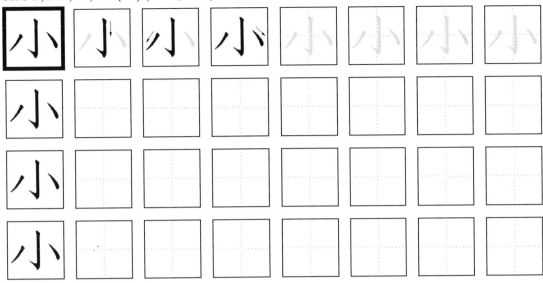

❷ **Dore desu-ka?** 月 日 木 本 人 大 小
Below each underlined part write the corresponding *kanji*. Use the correct stroke order. Check your answers by finding the words in the かんじノート sections of Lessons 7-9.

1. <u>moku</u>-yoo<u>bi</u>   6. <u>nihon-jin</u> [3 *kanji*]   11. ichi-<u>gatsu</u>   16. nan-<u>gatsu</u>

2. <u>shoogakkoo</u>   7. <u>oo</u>kii   12. <u>nichi</u>-yoo<u>bi</u>   17. <u>getsu</u>-yoo<u>bi</u>

3. futa<u>ri</u>   8. san-<u>nin</u>   13. <u>hon</u>   18. futsu<u>ka</u>

4. tanjoo<u>bi</u>   9. mai<u>nichi</u>   14. amerika-<u>jin</u>   19. <u>chii</u>sai

5. hito<u>ri</u>   10. <u>hito</u>   15. <u>daigaku</u>   20. juu-ichi-<u>nichi</u>

❸ **Kakimashoo!** 月 日 木 本 人 大 小
Read each of the following words aloud. Then underline the part(s) which you can write in *kanji*. Rewrite the entire word, substituting the known *kanji*. Use the correct stroke order. All of these words appear in ❷.

1. ひと   6. たんじょうび   11. ひとり   16. にほんじん

2. ほん   7. ちいさい   12. にちようび   17. もくようび

3. おおきい   8. じゅういちにち   13. さんにん   18. いちがつ

4. アメリカじん   9. ふたり   14. まいにち   19. ふつか

5. なんがつ   10. だいがく   15. げつようび   20. しょうがっこう

15

❹ **Dekimasu-ka?** 月 日 木 本 人 大 小

Read each of the following sentences aloud. Underline the part(s) which you can write in *kanji*. The number of known *kanji* in each sentence is given in brackets following the sentence. Copy the entire sentence substituting the known *kanji*. Check the textbook, かんじノート sections of Lessons 7-9.

1. この だいがくは おおきい です。 [2]

2. にちようびの パーティーに アメリカ人が ふたりと にほんじんが ろくにん

   きました。 [8]

3. ３がつ２３にちに にほんじんが ひとり しょうがっこうに きました。 [7]

4. もくようびに だいがくの ほんやで おおきい にほんごの ほんを かいました。

   わたしは このほんが だいすき です。 [10]

> **REMEMBER**
> The same *kanji* may have different readings – even within the same sentence.

❺ **More writing practice**

If you need additional practice, trace the sample *kanji* on the previous pages, and then use blank writing practice sheets.

LESSON 13
Daily School Life

PART 1
---

1. Read all of the notes for Lesson 13.

2. Learn the new vocabulary.

3. Yomimashoo!

Practice reading the following. Cover the *roomaji* side with a piece of paper and move it down one line at a time to check your accuracy. After you have finished, write the English equivalents in the right-hand column.

かなと かんじ	ローマじ	えいご
1. 小さい	chiisai	
2. 日本ごの本	nihongo-no hon	
3. 5日	itsuka	
4. なん月	nan-gatsu	
5. 日本	Nihon, Nippon	
6. 小学校	shoogakkoo	
7. 大すき	daisuki	
8. 月よう日	getsu-yoobi	
9. 4人	yo-nin	

16

かなと かんじ	ローマじ	えいご

10. カナダ人　　　　　kanada-jin

11. たんじょう日　　　tanjoobi

12. おとこの人　　　　otoko-no hito

13. 大学せい　　　　　daigakusei

14. 木よう日　　　　　moku-yoobi

15. 日本人　　　　　　nihon-jin

16. 日よう日　　　　　nichi-yoobi

17. ６月　　　　　　　roku-gatsu

PART 2

1. Watashi-no sukejuuru
Write six true sentences about your daily school schedule. Write each sentence in *kana (hiragana/katakana)*.
Use a number of different patterns, including those in the sample answers in the textbook, Interactive Activities
Part 1, ❷ of this lesson.

1. _____

2. _____

3. _____

4. _____

5. _____

6. _____

2. Preview the vocabulary and notes for Lesson 14.

LESSON 14
School Clubs

PART 1

1. Read all of the notes for Lesson 14.

2. Learn the new vocabulary.

3. Dekimasu-ka?
In each of the following sentences write the missing word in *hiragana*. All of the answers are *-te* forms of
verbs. Check your answers by finding the same sentences in the textbook, Interactive Activities Part 2, ❷ of
this lesson.

1. なかやまさんは _____ います。[eat]

2. ねこは ミルクを _____ います。[drink]

3. ゆかりさんは テレビを _____ います。[watch]

4. あきこちゃんは _____ います。[get up]

5. スミスさんは 日本ごぶに _____ います。 [join]

6. せんせいが _____ います。 [come]

7. せんせいは きょうしつに _____ います。 [enter]

8. たろうくんは ともだちと _____ います。 [speak]

9. あきこさんは _____ います。 [go to sleep]

10. まさよさんは うたを _____ います。 [sing]

Now make up one sentence of your own using *-te* form + *imasu*.

PART 2

1. Yomimashoo!

Practice reading the following. Cover the *roomaji* side with a piece of paper and move it down one line at a time to check your accuracy. After you have finished, write the English equivalents in the right-hand column.

かなと かんじ	ローマじ	えいご
1. 小さい	chiisai	
2. 日本ごの本	nihongo-no hon	
3. 5日	itsuka	
4. なん月	nan-gatsu	
5. 高い山	takai yama	
6. 小学校	shoogakkoo	
7. 大すき	daisuki	
8. 月よう日	getsu-yoobi	
9. 4人	yo-nin	
10. カナダ人	kanada-jin	
11. なん人	nan-nin	
12. おとこの人	otoko-no hito	
13. 中学校	chuugakkoo	
14. 木よう日	moku-yoobi	
15. 中に	naka-ni	
16. 日よう日	nichi-yoobi	
17. 6月	roku-gatsu	
18. 30日	san-juu-nichi	
19. 大きくない	ookikunai	
20. 高校せい	kookoosei	

18

2. Preview the vocabulary and notes for Lesson 15.

LESSON 15
Asking for and Giving Permission

PART 1

1. Read all of the notes for Lesson 15.

2. Learn the new vocabulary.

3. Yomimashoo!
Read each of the following sentences aloud, and then write the *roomaji* equivalent for the entire sentence under it. After you have finished all of the sentences, check your own work by looking at the sentences in the textbook, Interactive Activities Part 2, ❷ of this lesson.

1. その 大きい ホテルは 高い ですよ。

2. あの 高校は 小さい ですね。

3. ３月２５日は 日本の ともだちの たんじょう日です。

4. あの 人は 日本人 ですか。

5. あの 中学校の 中は きれい ですよ。

PART 2

1. Kakimashoo! 月 日 木 本 人 大 小
Read each of the following words aloud, and then write it, substituting the *kanji* which you have learned to write. Some of the words can be written entirely in *kanji*. Other words will include *hiragana* because they are normally written with *okurigana* or because you have not yet learned the corresponding *kanji*. Check your work by finding the words in the かんじノート sections of Lessons 7-9.

1. ひと

2. ほん

3. おおきい

4. にほんじん

5. ちいさい

6. もくようび

7. ３がつ

8. しょうがっこう

9. だいすき

10. みっか

2. Preview the vocabulary and notes for Lesson 16.

LESSON 16
More Spatial Relationships

1. Read all of the notes for Lesson 16.

2. Learn the new vocabulary.

3. Kakimashoo!
Practice writing the following *kanji* by reviewing Writing Practice ❶ in the lessons given below. With your pencil trace each *kanji* carefully, noting the correct stroke order. Then write each *kanji* at least five times on blank writing practice sheets. Count the strokes as you write the *kanji*. Review the readings also.

月、日 (Lesson 10)   木、本、人 (Lesson 11)   大、小 (Lesson 12)

1. Kakimashoo! 月 日 木 本 人 大 小
Read each of the following words aloud, and then write it, substituting the *kanji* which you have learned to write. Some of the words can be written entirely in *kanji*. Other words will include *hiragana* because they are normally written with *okurigana* or because you have not yet learned the corresponding *kanji*. Check your own work by finding the words in the かんじノート sections of Lessons 7-9.

1. にほんじん

2. もくようび

3. おおきい

4. ひと

5. しょうがっこう

6. ほん

7. ９がつ

8. ちいさい

9. だいがく

10. ふつか

2. Preview the vocabulary and notes for Lesson 17.

LESSON 17
Sequences of Daily Activities

1. Read all of the notes for Lesson 17.

2. Learn the new vocabulary.

3. Kakimashoo!
Use your imagination in this writing assignment, which provides you with additional practice in using the *-te* form to express a sequence of actions. You keep a *nikki* in which each day you always write only two sentences. The first sentence describes the **weather**. The second sentence lists the activities of the day. In the second sentence, include **at least five activities**. You always write everything in Japanese, including the **date** at the top of the page. Write the entry in the past tense. Use any *kanji* which you have learned how to write.

_____

_____

_____

_____

_____

_____

_____

_____

_____

_____

PART 2

1. Yomimashoo! 月 日 木 本 人 山 川 大 小 学 校 中 高 何
Read each of the following sentences aloud, and then write it in *roomaji*. Check your work by finding the same sentences in the textbook, かんじノート sections of the lessons given in brackets.

1. 何人 いますか。[17]

2. その 大きい ホテルは 高い ですよ。[15 Interactive Activities, Part 2, ❷]

3. 何の 本 ですか。[17]

4. ３月２５日は 日本の ともだちの たんじょう日です。[15 Interactive Activities, Part 2, ❷]

5. 木よう日に しました。[8]

6. 学校が みっつ あります。[13]

7. 中川さんは 小さい 大学に いきました。[14]

2. Preview the vocabulary and notes for Lesson 18.

LESSON 18
Weekend Activities

PART 1

1. Read all of the notes for Lesson 18.

2. Learn the new vocabulary.

3. Dekimasu-ka?
Can you unscramble the following sentence? Write the sentence in the correct order and then write what it means in English.

の 小さい かいました 私 今日 を 本 は 日本ご 。

1. Wakarimasu-ka?

What do the following sentences mean? Write in English.

1. 今日は 何も しません でした。　　1.

2. だれか アルバイト を しますか。　　2.

3. だれも いません。　　3.

4. あの 人は 何か よんで います。　　4.

5. つくえ の 中に 何も ありません。　　5.

6. だれか わかりますか。　　6.

2. Preview the vocabulary and notes for Lesson 19.

LESSON 19
Hobbies and Interests

PART 1

1. Read all of the notes for Lesson 19.

2. Learn the new vocabulary.

3. Complete Writing Practice ❶ Study, trace and write.

PART 2

1. Complete the remainder of the Writing Practice.

2. Preview the vocabulary and notes for Lesson 20.

WRITING PRACTICE

❶ **Study, trace and write.**

KA*; nan, nani (what, how many; *prefix to form questions*)

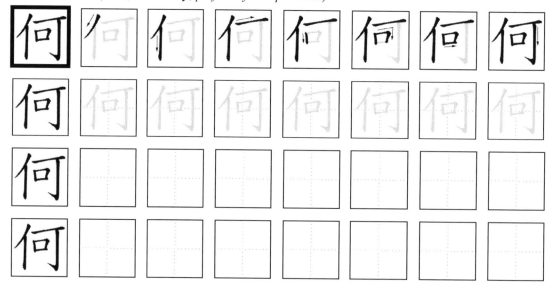

KON, KIN*; ima (now, the present)

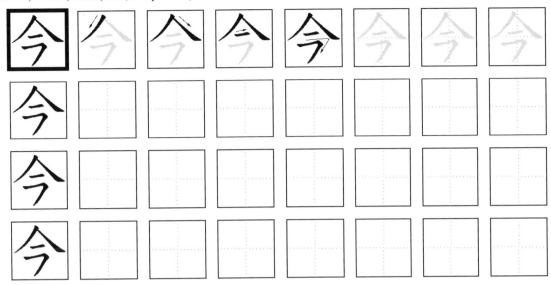

❷ **Dore desu-ka?**　月　日　木　本　人　大　小　何　今
Below each underlined part write the corresponding *kanji*. Use the correct stroke order. Check your answers by finding the words in the かんじノート sections of Lessons 7-18.

1. mai<u>nichi</u>	6. san-<u>nin</u>	11. <u>getsu</u>-yoo<u>bi</u>	16. <u>shoo</u>gakkoo
2. <u>hito</u>	7. <u>nan</u>-<u>gatsu</u>	12. <u>nan</u>-<u>nin</u>	17. <u>nan</u>-<u>nichi</u>
3. <u>dai</u>suki	8. tanjoo<u>bi</u>	13. <u>moku</u>-yoo<u>bi</u>	18. futa<u>ri</u>
4. <u>nihon</u>-<u>jin</u>	9. <u>hon</u>dana	14. <u>kyoo</u>	19. <u>oo</u>kii
5. <u>chii</u>sai	10. <u>ima</u>	15. itsu<u>ka</u>	20. <u>konnichi</u>-wa

❸ **Kakimashoo!**　月　日　木　本　人　大　小　何　今
Read each of the following words aloud. Then underline the part(s) which you can write in *kanji*. Rewrite the entire word, substituting the known *kanji*. Use the correct stroke order. All of these words appear in ❷.

1. ひと	6. たんじょうび	11. きょう	16. にほんじん
2. ほんだな	7. ちいさい	12. まいにち	17. もくようび
3. おおきい	8. こんにちは	13. さんにん	18. いま
4. なんにち	9. ふたり	14. なんにん	19. いつか
5. なんがつ	10. だいすき	15. げつようび	20. しょうがっこう

❹ **Dekimasu-ka?**　月　日　木　本　人　大　小　何　今

Read each of the following sentences aloud. Underline the part(s) which you can write in *kanji*. Copy the entire sentence, substituting the known *kanji*. The number of known *kanji* in each sentence is given in brackets following the sentence. Check the textbook, かんじノート sections of Lessons 7-9, 17 and 18.

1. あの ひとは にほんじん ですか。 [4]

2. げつようびは ともだちの たんじょうび です。 [3]

3. この にほんごの ほんが だいすき です。 [4]

4. トムさんは おおきい ねこと ちいさい いぬを かっています。 [2]

5. もくようびに ともだちが ふたり にほんに いきます。 [5]

❺ **More writing practice**

If you need additional practice, trace the sample *kanji* on the previous pages, and then use blank writing practice sheets.

LESSON 20
Writing to a Pen Pal

PART 1

1. Read all of the notes for Lesson 20.

2. Learn the new vocabulary.

3. Non-stop talking

Imagine that you are introducing yourself. Follow the usual procedure for non-stop talking and speak for two minutes about yourself. Then wait 30 seconds and speak again for two minutes. It is fine to repeat what you said during the first round, but you should be able to add more information the second time. Here is some information you might want to include.

Name	School subjects	Likes and dislikes
Age	Favorite subject	Friends
Birthday	Your family	Daily schedule
Grade	Your pets	Daily activities
School name	Your hobbies and interests	Weekend activities
Clubs you belong to	What you can and cannot do	Vacations

This assignment will help you to prepare for an activity in the next class.

PART 2

Kakimashoo!

Imagine that you are introducing yourself in a letter to a Japanese pen pal. Write at least one true sentence about yourself for each topic given. You may write in *kana/kanji* or in *roomaji*.

1. NAME _____

_____

2. AGE _____

_____

3. BIRTHDAY _____

_____

4. GRADE _____

_____

5. FAMILY _____

_____

6. PETS _____

_____

7. HOBBIES AND INTERESTS _____

_____

8. WEEKEND ACTIVITIES (Include at least three activities, and use the -*te* form.)

_____

_____

> *Kanji* you have learned to write: 月 日 木 本 人 大 小 何 今
> If you have successfully completed the Optional Writing Practices, you may also use
> any of these *kanji*: 山 川 学 校 中 高 私

REVIEW LESSON 1
Volume 1, Lessons 50-57

PART 1

1. Read all of the notes for Review Lesson 1.

2. Review the vocabulary.

3. Writing practice – What would you say?
Write what you would say in the following situations in *hiragana*. Write *gairaigo* in *katakana*.

1. You want to find out what days of the week your pen pal has geography class.

_____

2. Your history class is on Wednesdays and Fridays.

_____

3. You want to find out what sports your Japanese teacher likes the most.

_____

4. You are not really good at *karaoke*.

_____

PART 2

1. Writing gairaigo
Write the following items in *katakana* as you would with all *gairaigo*, then find its corresponding picture from below. Write the letter in the parentheses.

1. sakkaa _____ ( )   5. miruku _____ ( )

2. koora _____ ( )   6. pen _____ ( )

3. keeki _____ ( )   7. hotchikisu_____ ( )

4. koohii _____ ( )   8. fakkusu _____ ( )

a.   c.   e.   g.

b.   d.   f.   h.

2. Dialogue

Read the following dialogue between Keiko and Miho and answer the questions in English.

Keiko: みほさん、 ゴルフが できますか。
Miho: はい、 へたですけど、 すきですよ。
Keiko: じゃ、 どようびに いっしょに
　　　 ゴルフを しませんか。
Miho: あ、 いいですね。 しましょう。
　　　 なんじに しましょうか。
Keiko: ２じに しませんか。
Miho: はい、 そうしましょう。

1. What kind of sport are they talking about?
_____

2. Did Miho say she's good at this sport?
_____

3. Does she like this sport?
_____

4. Which day of the week are they going to play this sport? _____

5. What time are they going to play this sport? _____

3. Nihongo-de kaite kudasai.

Describe the following. Finish the following sentences choosing the appropriate adjectives from the box below. Make sure to put the letter in the parentheses to indicate which adjective you have selected.

1. ぼく／わたしの まちは _____。 ( )

2. カラオケは _____。 ( )

3. にほんごの じゅぎょうは _____。 ( )

4. がっこうの コンピューターは _____。 ( )

5. ぼく／わたしの かばんは _____。 ( )

a. small	e. easy	i. slow	m. delicious
b. big	f. interesting	j. new	n. red
c. quiet	g. boring	k. old	o. black
d. difficult	h. fast	l. good	p. blue

REVIEW LESSON 2
Volume 1, Lessons 58-66

PART 1

1. Read all of the notes for Review Lesson 2.

2. Review the vocabulary.

3. Writing practice – What would you say?
Write what you would say in the following situations in *hiragana*.

1. When you want to ask your friend which clothes you should get.

_____

2. When you decide on getting something, such as some item you are looking at.

_____

3. When you want to ask what this weekend's weather will be like.

_____

4. When you tell someone it looks like rain tomorrow.

_____

PART 2

1. Katakana writing practice
Re-write the following *katakana* words, then write their English equivalents on the lines.

1. コンピューター

2. チョコレート

3. ジュース

4. ワイン

5. ナイフ

6. ベッド

7. ボタン

8. レモン

2. Reading practice
Read the following passage. Then answer the questions that follow in English.

しゅうまつ あねと デパートに かいものに いきました。あねは くろいくつと むらさきの くつしたを かいました。くつしたは 900えん でした。ちょっと たかい ですけど、とても きれい です。わたしは かわいい ブラウスと みどりの スカート を かいました。

1. Who did the writer go shopping with? _____

2. Where did they go shopping? _____

3. What did the writer buy? (list both items) _____

4. What did the other person buy? (list both items) _____

REVIEW LESSON 3
Volume 1, Lessons 67-73

PART 1
---

1. Read all of the notes for Review Lesson 3.

2. Review the vocabulary.

3. Writing practice – What would you say?
Write what you would say in the following situations in *hiragana*.

1. When you want to ask how someone will go to a party.

_____

2. When your want to suggest that you and your friend go by subway.

_____

3. When you want to say that Mr. Hayashi is inside the bookstore now.

_____

4. When you want to ask if the post office is nearby.

_____

5. When you want to ask how long it takes to get there on foot.

_____

PART 2

Reading practice
A. Read the following descriptions about the family photo and write the name in the parentheses under each person. Write in English.

わたしの なまえは ウェンディーです。
わたしの みぎに ははが います。
ははの なまえは ナンシーです。
わたしの ひだりに ちちが います。
ちちの なまえは ジム です。
ははの うしろに あにが います。
あにの なまえは トムです。
いもうとは あにの ひだりに います。
いもうとの なまえは アリスです。

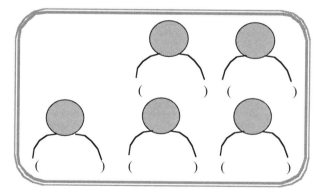

B. Answer the questions in Japanese.

1. おかあさんの うしろに だれが いますか。　　　　　_____が います。

2. いもうとさんの まえに だれが いますか。　　　　　_____が います。

3. ウェンディーさんの みぎに だれが いますか。　　　_____が います。

4. おにいさんの ひだりに だれが いますか。　　　　　_____が います。

REVIEW LESSON 4
Volume 2, Lessons 6-15

PART 1
---

1. Read all of the notes for Review Lesson 4.

2. Review the vocabulary.

3. Writing practice – What would you say?
Write what you would say in the following situations in *hiragana* (and *kanji* where possible).

1. When you want to ask what the date (month and day of the month) is.

_____

2. When you want to ask what club someone belongs to.

_____

3. When you want to request that someone say something again slowly.

_____

4. When you want to ask someone to give you his/her phone number.

_____

5. When you want to ask permission to use this textbook.

_____

PART 2
---

1. Sentence completion
Fill in the blanks with the correct geographical terms and names of places.

1. 日本で いちばん 大きい_____は _____です。[island]
　 せいかいで いちばん 大きいのは _____です。

2. 日本で いちばん高い _____は _____です。[mountain]
　 アメリカで いちばん 高いのは _____です。

3. アメリカで いちばん ながい_____は _____です。[river]
　 せかいで いちばん ながいのは _____です。

4. 日本で いちばん 大きい _____は _____です。[lake]
　 アメリカで いちばん 大きいのは _____です。

2. Reading practice

Read the dialog below between Yuka and her older brother, Kenji. Then answer the questions that follow in English.

Yuka: おにいちゃんの 学校の ともだちの マリウスさんは どちらから?
Kenji: カナダから だよ。
Yuka: へえ。 カナダの どちらから?
Kenji: カナダの ケベックから。
Yuka: ああ、 そう。 マリウスさんは なにごを はなすの?
Kenji: フランスごと えいごを はなすよ。
Yuka: にほんごは?
Kenji: にほんごも すこし できるよ。
Yuka: わあ、 かっこいい!

1. Where did Kenji meet his friend Marius? _____

2. What country is Marius from? _____

3. What language(s) does he speak? _____

4. What does Yuka think about him? _____

REVIEW LESSON 5
Volume 2, Lessons 16-20

PART 1

1. Read all of the notes for Review Lesson 5.

2. Review the vocabulary.

3. Writing practice – What would you say?

Write what you would say in the following situations in *hiragana* (and *kanji* where possible).

1. When you return home. _____

    To which the response would be: _____

2. When you are leaving the house. _____

    To which the response would be: _____

3. When you want to say [there was a meeting but] <u>no one came</u>.

    _____

4. When you want to ask someone what his/her hobbies are.

    _____

5. When you tell someone you didn't eat anything.

    _____

6. When you want to ask your friend if they will have something to drink.

    _____

7. You are visiting your friend, Mariko, and want to comment on how neat her room is.

    _____

1. Reading comprehension

Read the following passage about Mike's hobby and answer the questions that follow in English.

ぼくの しゅみは まんがを あつめる ことと えいがを みる こと です。
アメリカの ふるい まんがが すき ですけど 日本の まんがも すき です。
えいがは アクションえいがが いちばん すき です。よく ガールフレンドと
えいがを みます。ガールフレンドは ラブストーリーが すき です。

1. What two hobbies does Mike have?

_____

2. What is his preference regarding his first hobby?

_____

3. What is his preference regarding his second hobby?

_____

4. Who does he often go with to enjoy his second hobby?

_____

5. What is her preference?

_____

2. Sentence writing practice

Write sentences about tomorrow's plans using the following hints, as in the example.

Ex. listen to _____, and read _____ → ジャズをきいて、ざっしをよみます。

1. wake up at _____, and drink _____ → _____

2. meet _____, and go to _____ → _____

3. go to _____, and buy _____ → _____

4. return home, and do _____ → _____

5. write a letter to _____, and go to bed at _____

  → _____

3. Preview the vocabulary and notes for Lesson 21.

LESSON 21
Writing a Letter to a Friend

1. Read all of the notes for Lesson 21.

2. Learn the new vocabulary.

3. Yomimashoo!

Practice reading the letter in the textbook, Interactive Activities Part 2, ❶. Read the *roomaji* version aloud twice. Then mask the *roomaji* version as you read the letter in Japanese. Uncover the *roomaji* line by line to check your accuracy. Repeat this assignment until you can read the entire letter in Japanese within one minute.

1. Tegami-o kakimashoo!
Imagine that you are writing a letter in Japanese to a Japanese friend. Follow the directions in the box below. You may write in *kana/kanji* or in *roomaji*.

TOMODACHI-NI TEGAMI-O KAKIMASHOO!

Write the month, day, and weather at the top. In the body of the letter write about one or more of your activities. You can include information on:

    1. When and where you went
    2. How you went there
    3. What you did
    4. With whom you did the activity
    5. What kind of activity it was (interesting movie, fun party, etc.)

You may wish to include some comments on the weather. Refer to the letter in the textbook, Interactive Activities Part 2, ❶ for ideas on how to begin and end your letter.

Kanji you have learned to write: 月 日 木 本 人 大 小 何 今
If you have successfully completed the Optional Writing Practices, you may also use any of these *kanji*: 山 川 学 校 中 高 私 天 元 気

2. Preview the vocabulary and notes for Lesson 22.

LESSON 22
Seasons and Activities

1. Read all of the notes for Lesson 22.

2. Learn the new vocabulary.

3. Complete Writing Practice ❶ Study, trace and write.

1. **Complete the remainder of the Writing Practice.**

2. **Preview the vocabulary and notes for Lesson 23.**

WRITING PRACTICE

❶ **Study, trace and write.**

KA; hi* [bi]* (fire)

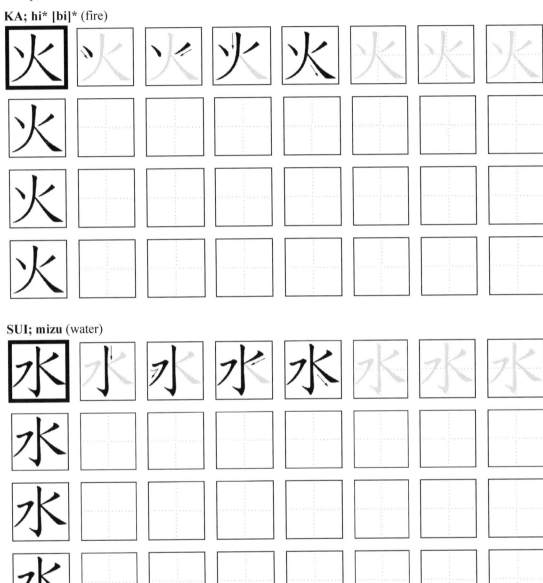

SUI; mizu (water)

❷ **Dore desu-ka?** 月 日 木 本 人 大 小 何 今 火 水
Below each underlined part write the corresponding *kanji*. Use the correct stroke order. Check your answers by
finding the words in the かんじノート sections of Lessons 7-9, 17, 18, and 20.

1. o-<u>mizu</u>   6. yo-<u>nin</u>   11. <u>ka</u>-yoo<u>bi</u>   16. <u>shoogakkoo</u>

2. <u>hito</u>   7. <u>nan-gatsu</u>   12. <u>nan-nin</u>   17. <u>nan-nichi</u>

3. <u>daigaku</u>   8. <u>sui</u>yoo<u>bi</u>   13. <u>moku</u>-yoo<u>bi</u>   18. <u>futari</u>

4. <u>nihon-jin</u>   9. <u>hon</u>   14. <u>kyoo</u>   19. <u>ookii</u>

5. <u>chiisai</u>   10. <u>ima</u>   15. <u>futsuka</u>   20. <u>konnichi</u>-wa

❸ **Kakimashoo!** 月 日 木 本 人 大 小 何 今 火 水
Read each of the following words aloud. Then underline the part(s) which you can write in *kanji*. Rewrite the
entire word, substituting the known *kanji*. Use the correct stroke order. All of these words appear in ❷.

1. ひと   6. すいようび   11. きょう   16. にほんじん

2. ほん   7. ちいさい   12. おみず   17. もくようび

3. おおきい   8. こんにちは   13. よにん   18. いま

4. なんにち   9. ふたり   14. なんにん   19. ふつか

5. なんがつ   10. だいがく   15. かようび   20. しょうがっこう

❹ **Dekimasu-ka?** 月 日 木 本 人 大 小 何 今 火 水
Read each of the following sentences aloud. Underline the part(s) which you can write in *kanji*. Copy the
entire sentence, substituting the known *kanji*. The number of known *kanji* in each sentence is given in brackets
following the sentence. Also check the textbook, かんじノート sections of Lessons 7-9 and 17, 18 and 20.

1. あのひとは カナダじん ですか。 [2]

2. きょうは かようび です。 [4]

3. あのだいがくの にほんごの せんせいは にほんじん じゃない です。 [6]

4. げつようびと かようびと すいようびは はれ でした。 もくようびは あめ

   でした。 [8]

5. いま なんじ ですか。 [2]

6. わたしの くるまは ちいさい ですけど、 だいすき です。 [2]

7. ここの おみずは おいしい です。[1]

❺ **More writing practice**
If you need additional practice, trace the sample *kanji* on the previous pages, and then use blank writing practice sheets.

LESSON 23
Talking about a Trip

PART 1
---

1. Read all of the notes for Lesson 23.

2. Complete Writing Practice ❶ Study, trace and write.

PART 2
---

1. Complete the remainder of the Writing Practice.

2. Preview the vocabulary and notes for Lesson 24.

WRITING PRACTICE

❶ **Study, trace and write.**

KIN, KON* (gold); **kane** (money)

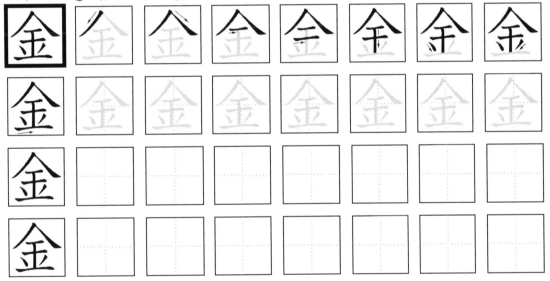

35

DO, TO*; tsuchi* (earth, soil)

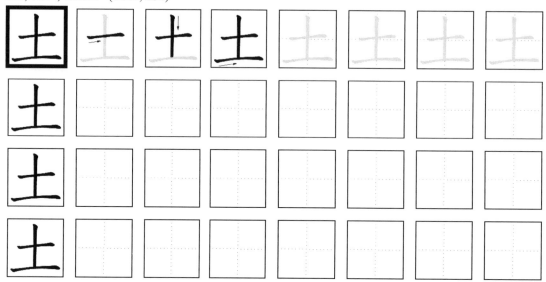

❷ **Dore desu-ka?** 月 日 木 本 人 大 小 何 今 火 水 金 土
Below each underlined part write the corresponding *kanji*. Use the correct stroke order. Check your answers by finding the words in the かんじノート sections of Lessons 7-9, 17, 18, and 20.

1. nan-gatsu
2. ookii
3. ima
4. konnichi-wa
5. chiisai

6. san-nin
7. kin-yoobi
8. o-mizu
9. nan-nin
10. daisuki

11. o-kane
12. hondana
13. ka-yoobi
14. kyoo
15. do-yoobi

16. shoogakkoo
17. nan-nichi
18. sui-yoobi
19. hito
20. nihon-jin

❸ **Kakimashoo!** 月 日 木 本 人 大 小 何 今 火 水 金 土
Read each of the following words aloud. Then underline the part(s) which you can write in *kanji*. Rewrite the entire word, substituting the known *kanji*. Use the correct stroke order. All of these words appear in ❷.

1. ちいさい
2. ほんだな
3. おおきい
4. なんにち
5. なんがつ

6. おみず
7. ひと
8. こんにちは
9. すいようび
10. だいすき

11. きょう
12. きんようび
13. いま
14. なんにん
15. おかね

16. にほんじん
17. かようび
18. さんにん
19. どようび
20. しょうがっこう

❹ **Dekimasu-ka?** 月 日 木 本 人 大 小 何 今 火 水 金 土
Read each of the following sentences aloud. Underline the part(s) which you can write in *kanji*. Copy the entire sentence, substituting the known *kanji*. The number of known *kanji* in each sentence is given in brackets following the sentence. Check the textbook, かんじノート sections of Lessons 7-9 and 17, 18 and 20.

1. きょうは なんようび ですか。[4]

2. きんようびが すき です。[2]

3. かようびと すいようびは ゆきでした。[4]

4. だいがくに にほんごの せんせいが ふたり います。[4]

5. どようびと にちようびは うちで にほんごの べんきょうを します。[6]

❺ **More writing practice**
If you need additional practice, trace the sample *kanji* on the previous pages, and then use blank writing practice sheets.

LESSON 24
Telephoning

PART 1

1. Read all of the notes for Lesson 24.

2. Learn the new vocabulary.
Study the vocabulary in both the たんご and たんごノート sections.

PART 2

1. Rusuban denwa-no messeeji
You are calling Japanese friends to invite them to join you for some activity tomorrow. Write down the message which you will leave on the るすばんでんわ of those ともだち who are not home. Include enough information that your friends will want to join you and will respond to your request to call you back. Refer back to the message you wrote for the textbook activity in Interactive Activities Part 2, ❷, but **do not use the same message**.

_____

_____

_____

_____

_____

_____

_____

2. Preview the vocabulary and notes for Lesson 25.

LESSON 25
Expressing Wants

1. Read all of the notes for Lesson 25.

2. Learn the new vocabulary.

3. Yasumi-ni nani-o shitai desu-ka?
Write three different answers to this question in *kana/kanji* or in *roomaji*. Be sure to use the *-tai* form of the verb (*shitai, ikitai, mitai, yomitai,* etc.). This assignment will help prepare you for the textbook, Interactive Activities Part 2, ❷.

1. _____

2. _____

3. _____

1. Yomimashoo!
Read each of the following aloud, and then write the equivalent in *hiragana* or in *roomaji*.

1. 天気

2. 何月何日

3. 火よう日

4. 元気

5. 金よう日

6. お水

7. 私

8. 土よう日

9. お金

10. 水よう日

11. 日本人

12. 木よう日

13. ３月

14. 小さい小学校

15. 今月

2. Preview the vocabulary and notes for Lesson 26.

LESSON 26
Admission Prices

1. Read all of the notes for Lesson 26.

2. Learn the new vocabulary.

3. Kanji review
Practice writing the following *kanji* by reviewing Writing Practice ❶ in the lessons given below. With your pencil trace each *kanji* carefully, noting the correct stroke order. Review the readings also.

月、日 (Lesson 10)   木、本、人 (Lesson 11)   大、小 (Lesson 12)

4. Kakimashoo! 月 日 木 本 人 大 小
Read each of the following words aloud, and then write it, substituting the *kanji* which you have learned to write. Some of the words can be written entirely in *kanji*. Other words will include *hiragana* because they are normally written with *okurigana* or because you have not yet learned the corresponding *kanji*. Check your own work by finding the words in the かんじノート sections of Lessons 7-9.

1. にほんじん	6. ほん	11. おおさか
2. もくようび	7. ひとり	12. さんにん
3. おおきい	8. ちいさい	13. しょうがっこう
4. ひと	9. だいがく	14. 9 がつ
5. げつようび	10. ふつか	15. だいすき

PART 2

1. Kanji review

Practice writing the following *kanji* by reviewing Writing Practice ❶ in the lessons given below. With your pencil trace each *kanji* carefully, noting the correct stroke order. Then write each *kanji* at least four times on blank writing practice sheets. Count the strokes as you write the *kanji*. Review the readings also.

何、今 (Lesson 19)   火、水 (Lesson 22)   金、土 (Lesson 23)

2. Kakimashoo! 月 日 木 本 人 大 小 何 今 火 水 金 土

Read each of the following words aloud, and then write it, substituting the *kanji* which you have learned to write. Some of the words can be written entirely in *kanji*. Other words will include *hiragana* because they are normally written with *okurigana* or because you have not yet learned the corresponding *kanji*. Check your work by finding the words in the かんじノート sections of Lessons 17, 18, and 20.

1. なに	6. なんようび	11. すいようび
2. いま	7. おかね	12. なんにん
3. かようび	8. どようび	13. こんげつ
4. おみず	9. なんにち	14. きょう
5. きんようび	10. こんにちは	15. なんのほんですか。

3. Preview the vocabulary and notes for Lesson 27.

LESSON 27
Sporting Events

PART 1

1. Read all of the notes for Lesson 27.

2. Learn the new vocabulary.

3. Dekimasu-ka?

Write the following sentences in *roomaji*, leaving space between the words and affixing the particles to the preceding nouns. Then write the English equivalent for each sentence.

1. いつじゅうどうのれんしゅうをしますか。

2. きのうのやきゅうのしあいはライオンズがかちましたか。

PART 2

1. Kakimashoo!

Use your imagination to complete the following passage. Choose the name of a team from those listed in the chart in the textbook, Interactive Activities Part 2, ❷. Write everything in *kana*. Refer to the *Katakana* Chart to help you write the team's name. Vocabulary for different sports can be found in Volume 1 of the textbook, Lessons 53-55.

_____ の チームは _____ が いちばん すき です。
(supootsu-no namae)　　　　　　　　(chiimu-no namae)

_____ です。_____ の しあいは _____ が
(tsuyoi/yowai)　　　　(kinoo/senshuu/moku-yoobi/senshuu-no getsu-yoobi/etc.)　　　　(chiimu-no namae)

_____。スコアは _____ でした。
(kachimashita/makemashita)　　　　　　　(# tai #)

2. Preview the vocabulary and notes for Lesson 28.

LESSON 28
Leisure Time

PART 1

1. Read all of the notes for Lesson 28.

2. Learn the new vocabulary.

3. Complete Writing Practice ❶ Study, trace and write.

PART 2

1. Complete the remainder of the Writing Practice.

2. Preview the vocabulary and notes for Lesson 29.

WRITING PRACTICE
❶ **Study, trace and write.**

KEN*; mi(ru) (see, look at, watch)

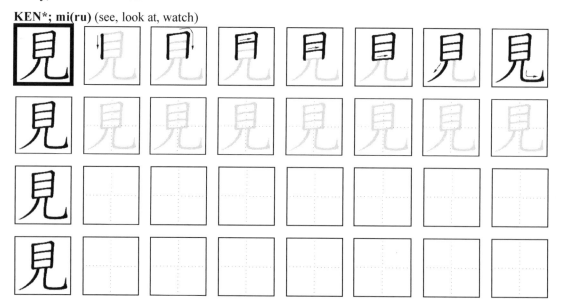

40

KOO*, GYOO*; i(ku) (go), **yu(ki)*** (bound for)

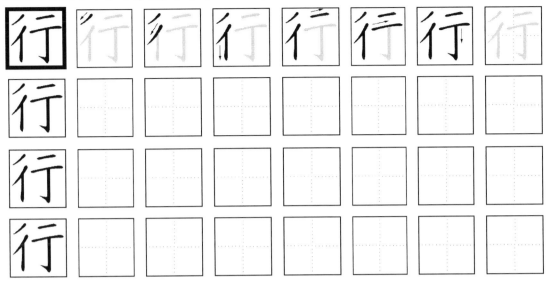

❷ **Dore desu-ka?** 月 日 木 本 人 大 小 何 今 火 水 金 土 見 行
Below each underlined part write the corresponding *kanji*. Use the correct stroke order. Check your answers by finding the words in the textbook, かんじノート sections of Lessons 7-9, 17, 18, 20 and 27.

1. o-<u>mizu</u>

2. <u>oo</u>kii

3. <u>nan-nin</u>

4. <u>nihon-jin</u>

5. itsu<u>ka</u>

6. kyuu-<u>nin</u>

7. <u>nan-gatsu</u>

8. <u>iki</u>mashita

9. o-<u>kane</u>

10. <u>nan-nichi</u>

11. <u>getsu</u>-yoo<u>bi</u>

12. <u>daisuki</u>

13. <u>moku</u>-yoo<u>bi</u>

14. <u>kyoo</u>

15. <u>chii</u>sai

16. <u>shoogakkoo</u>

17. <u>ima</u>

18. <u>mite</u>-imasu

19. <u>hito</u>

20. <u>konnichi</u>-wa

❸ **Kakimashoo!** 月 日 木 本 人 大 小 何 今 火 水 金 土 見 行
Read each of the following words aloud. Then underline the part(s) which you can write in *kanji*. Rewrite the entire word, substituting the known *kanji*. Use the correct stroke order. All of these words appear in ❷.

1. ひと

2. おかね

3. おおきい

4. なんにち

5. なんがつ

6. いきました

7. ちいさい

8. こんにちは

9. みています

10. だいすき

11. きょう

12. おみず

13. きゅうにん

14. なんにん

15. げつようび

16. にほんじん

17. もくようび

18. いま

19. いつか

20. しょうがっこう

41

❹ **Dekimasu-ka?** 月 日 木 本 人 大 小 何 今 火 水 金 土 見 行
Read each of the following sentences aloud. Underline the part(s) which you can write in *kanji*. Copy the entire sentence, substituting the known *kanji*. The number of known *kanji* in each sentence is given in brackets following the sentence. Check the textbook, かんじノート sections of Lessons 7-9, 17, 18, 20, and 27.

1. まいにち にほんの テレビを みます。 [4]

2. いま なんの ほんを よんでいますか。 [3]

3. ３がつ １９にちは アメリカの ともだちの たんじょうび です。 [3]

4. トムさんは おおきい ねこと ちいさい いぬを かっています。 [2]

5. きょうは えいがを みて ひるごはんを たべて ドライブに いく。 [4]

6. もくようびに ともだちが ふたり にほんに いきます。 [6]

❺ **More writing practice**
If you need additional practice, trace the sample *kanji* on the previous pages, and then use blank writing practice sheets.

LESSON 29
Having a Party

PART 1
---

1. Read all of the notes for Lesson 29.

2. Learn the new vocabulary.

3. Dekimasu-ka?
Can you unscramble the following sentence? Write the sentence in the correct order and then write what it means in English.

うち の に きません に か わたし あそび 。

PART 2
---

1. Shitsumon-ni kotaete kudasai.
Write answers to the following questions about the dialogue in the textbook, Interactive Activities Part 2, ❶. Write in *kana/kanji*.

1. だれが でんわを しましたか。

2. パーティーは いつ ですか。

3. 高山さんは ひま ですか。

4. だれが パーティーに 来ますか。

5. パーティーは 何じから ですか。

2. Preview the vocabulary and notes for Lesson 30.

LESSON 30
Review

PART 1
---

1. Read all of the notes for Lesson 30.

2. Review the negative of the plain form.
Write the negative counterpart for each of the plain form verbs below. Check your own work by referring to the chart in the ぶんぽうポイント section of the textbook, Lesson 28. Look at the examples.

*NON-PAST PLAIN FORM					
Affirmative	**English**	**Negative**	**Affirmative**	**English**	**Negative**
1. iu	say	iwanai	10. nomu		
2. akeru	open	akenai	11. wasureru		
3. kaku	write	kakanai	12. aru		
4. yomu			13. oshieru		
5. taberu			14. kiku		
6. miru			15. kau		
7. suru			16. hairu		
8. wakaru			17. kaeru		
9. iku					

PART 2
---

1. Wakarimasu-ka?
What do the following sentences mean? Write in English.

1. きょ年は 何を しましたか。

2. 来しゅうの 天気は どう ですか。

3. せんしゅうの 月よう日に 来ました。

4. 今日 私は いそがしい です。

5. 今月は 五月 じゃ ない です。

6. 今年も せかい りょこうを したい です。

2. Preview the vocabulary and notes for Lesson 31.

LESSON 31
Review

1. Read all of the notes for Lesson 31.

2. Kanji review

For each *kanji* write the readings you have learned as well as the meaning(s) in English. Check your own work by finding the answers in the かんじノート sections of the textbook indicated after each *kanji*.

	KANJI	READINGS	MEANING(S)
1	月 [7]		
2	日 [7]		
3	木 [8]		
4	本 [8]		
5	人 [8]		
6	山 [8]		
7	川 [8]		
8	大 [9]		
9	小 [9]		
10	学 [13]		
11	校 [13]		
12	中 [14]		
13	高 [14]		
14	何 [17]		
15	今 [18]		
16	私 [18]		
17	火 [20]		
18	水 [20]		
19	金 [20]		
20	土 [20]		
21	天 [21]		
22	元 [21]		
23	気 [21]		
24	田 [24]		
25	見 [27]		
26	行 [27]		
27	来 [29]		
28	年 [29]		

3. Preview the vocabulary and notes for Lesson 32.

LESSON 32
Reviewing Counting and Prices

PART 1
---

1. Read all of the notes for Lesson 32.

2. Learn the new vocabulary.
In addition to the words, phrases, and expressions in the 単語 (Vocabulary) section, be sure to review the counters and the numbers in the 文法ポイント (Key Grammar Points) section of the textbook.

3. Prepare for an interactive activity.
Prepare the materials needed for the textbook, Interactive Activities Part 2, ❶.

4. Yomimashoo!
Write the *hiragana* or *roomaji* equivalent of each of the following counters.

1. 八つ   4. 九つ   7. 三つ

2. 六つ   5. 四つ   8. 一つ

3. 二つ   6. 七つ   9. 五つ

PART 2
---

1. Yomimashoo!
Read each of the following aloud, and then write the equivalent in *hiragana* or in *roomaji*.

1. 何を 見て いますか。 ➜

2. 来月は 山に 行きたい です。 ➜

3. どっちが 大きい ですか。 ➜

4. この 小さい本を 見て ください。 ➜

5. 来年 日本から 田中さんが 来ます。 ➜

2. Preview the vocabulary and notes for Lesson 33.

LESSON 33
Nearby Locations

PART 1
---

1. Read all of the notes for Lesson 33.

2. Learn the new vocabulary.
In addition to studying the words, phrases, and expressions in the 単語 section, be sure to practice the counter - *mai* when combined with different numbers (in the 文法ポイント section).

3. Kakimashoo! 月 日 木 本 人 大 小
Read each of the following words aloud, and then write it, substituting the *kanji* which you have learned to write. Some of the words can be written entirely in *kanji*. Other words will include *hiragana* because they are normally written with *okurigana* or because you have not yet learned the corresponding *kanji*. Check your work by finding the words in the かんじノート sections of the textbook, Lessons 7-9.

1. にほんじん	6. ほん	11. おおさか
2. もくようび	7. ひとり	12. さんにん
3. おおきい	8. ちいさい	13. しょうがっこう
4. ひと	9. だいがく	14. 9がつ
5. げつようび	10. ふつか	15. だいすき

PART 2

1. Kanji review

Practice writing the following *kanji* by reviewing Writing Practice ❶ in the lessons given below. With your pencil trace each *kanji* carefully, noting the correct stroke order. Then write each *kanji* at least three times on blank writing practice sheets. Count the strokes as you write the *kanji*. Review the readings also.

何、今 (Lesson 19)　火、水 (Lesson 22)　金、土 (Lesson 23)　見、行 (Lesson 28)

2. Kakimashoo! 月 日 木 本 人 大 小 何 今 火 水 金 土 見 行

Read each of the following words aloud, and then write it, substituting the *kanji* which you have learned to write. Some of the words can be written entirely in *kanji*. Other words will include *hiragana* because they are normally written with *okurigana* or because you have not yet learned the corresponding *kanji*. Check your work by finding the words in the textbook, かんじノート sections of Lessons 17, 18 and 20.

1. なに	6. なんようび	11. すいようび
2. いま	7. おかね	12. なんにん
3. かようび	8. どようび	13. こんげつ
4. おみず	9. なんにち	14. きょう
5. きんようび	10. こんにちは	15. なんのほんですか。

3. Preview the vocabulary and notes for Lesson 34.

LESSON 34
More Spatial Relationships

PART 1

1. Read all of the notes for Lesson 34.

2. Complete Writing Practice ❶ Study, trace and write.

3. Kakimashoo!

You are buying three dozen doughnuts for a party. You have decided on the six kinds of doughnuts shown below (A - F) in the rack which is behind the salesperson. They are not labeled so you must tell the salesperson which ones you want <u>and</u> how many of each. You buy different numbers of the different kinds. Write one sentence for each kind of doughnut, showing what you say to the salesperson. **Write in *kana*.** Use ordinal numbers (*ichi-ban-me, ni-ban-me, san-ban-me*, etc.) and the spatial relationship words *migi* and *hidari*. Look at the example.

ドーナッツ

		B	D		A		E		C			F	

Ex. (C) みぎから 五ばんめの ドーナッツを 三つ ください。

1. ( ) _____

2. ( ) _____

3. ( ) _____

4. ( ) _____

5. ( ) _____

PART 2

1. Complete the remainder of the Writing Practice section.

2. Preview the vocabulary and notes for Lesson 35.

WRITING PRACTICE

❶ **Study, trace and write.**

GAKU (learning, science); **mana(bu)*** (learn)

KOO (school)

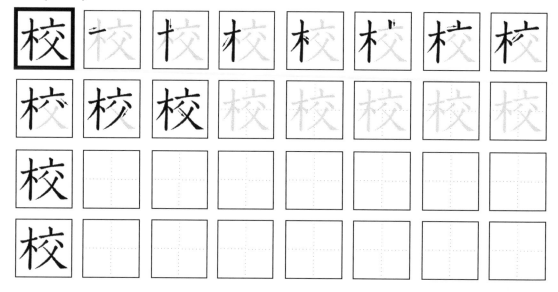

❷ **Dore desu-ka?** 月 日 木 本 人 大 小 何 今 火 水 金 土 見 行 学 校
Below each underlined part write the corresponding *kanji*. Use the correct stroke order. Check your answers by finding the words in the textbook, かんじノート sections of Lessons 7-9, 13, 17, 18, 20, and 27.

1. <u>chii</u>sai

2. <u>kyoo</u>

3. koo<u>koo</u>

4. <u>shoogakkoo</u>

5. <u>mi</u>mashita

6. <u>ikimasen</u>

7. nan-<u>gatsu</u>

8. hachi-<u>nin</u>

9. <u>nihon-jin</u>

10. <u>moku-yoobi</u>

11. <u>getsu-yoobi</u>

12. <u>daigaku</u>

13. nan-<u>nichi</u>

14. <u>ookii</u>

15. o-<u>mizu</u>

16. o-<u>kane</u>

17. <u>mi</u>te-imasu

18. <u>ima</u>

19. <u>konnichi</u>-wa

20. <u>hito</u>

❸ **Kakimashoo!** 月 日 木 本 人 大 小 何 今 火 水 金 土 見 行 学 校
Read each of the following words aloud. Then underline the part(s) which you can write in *kanji*. Rewrite the entire word, substituting the known *kanji*. Use the correct stroke order. All of these words appear in section ❷.

1. ひと

2. おかね

3. おおきい

4. なんにち

5. なんがつ

6. いきません

7. ちいさい

8. こんにちは

9. みています

10. だいがく

11. きょう

12. おみず

13. はちにん

14. こうこう

15. げつようび

16. にほんじん

17. もくようび

18. いま

19. みました

20. しょうがっこう

❹ Dekimasu-ka? 月 日 木 本 人 大 小 何 今 火 水 金 土 見 行 学 校

Read each of the following sentences aloud. Underline the part(s) which you can write in *kanji*. Copy the entire sentence, substituting the known *kanji*. The number of known *kanji* in each sentence is given in brackets following the sentence. Also check the textbook, かんじノート sections of Lessons 7-9, 13, 17, 18, 20, and 27.

1. この ちかくに だいがくが ありますか。[2]

2. ジェシカさんは ちいさい いぬと おおきい ねこを かっています。[2]

3. きょうは どこに いきたいですか。[3]

4. どようびに なんの えいがを みましたか。[4]

5. こんげつの１９にちは すいようびです。[5]

6. きんようびに がっこうの ともだちが にほんに いきます。[7]

❺ More writing practice

If you need additional practice, trace the sample *kanji* on the previous pages, and then use blank writing practice sheets.

LESSON 35
Numbers up to 100,000

PART 1
---

1. Read all of the notes for Lesson 35.

2. Learn the new vocabulary.

3. Complete Writing Practice ❷ Study, trace and write.

PART 2
---

1. Complete the remainder of the Writing Practice.

2. Preview the vocabulary and notes for Lesson 36.

WRITING PRACTICE

❶ Dore desu-ka? 月 日 木 本 人 大 小 何 今 火 水 金 土 見 行 学 校 中 高

Below each underlined part write the corresponding *kanji*. Use the correct stroke order. Check your answers by finding the words in the textbook, かんじノート sections of Lessons 7-9, 13, 14, 17, 18, 20, and 27.

1. takai	6. konnichi-wa	11. ookii	16. kookoo
2. hito	7. nan-gatsu	12. moku-yoobi	17. ima
3. nan-nin	8. mimasen	13. daigaku	18. iku
4. o-mizu	9. o-kane	14. kyoo	19. nihon-jin
5. naka	10. chuugakkoo	15. chiisai	20. shichi-nin

❷ **Study, trace and write.**

CHUU; naka (middle, inside, within)

KOO; taka(i) (high, expensive)

❸ **Kakimashoo!** 月 日 木 本 人 大 小 何 今 火 水 金 土 見 行 学 校 中 高
Read each of the following words aloud. Then underline the part(s) which you can write in *kanji*. Rewrite the entire word, substituting the known *kanji*. Use the correct stroke order. All of these words appear in section ❶.

1. なんにん

2. いま

3. こうこう

4. ちゅうがっこう

5. なんがつ

6. いく

7. ちいさい

8. こんにちは

9. みません

10. だいがく

11. きょう

12. おみず

13. しちにん

14. ひと

15. たかい

16. にほんじん

17. もくようび

18. おかね

19. なか

20. おおきい

❹ Dekimasu-ka?
Read each of the following sentences aloud. Underline the part(s) which you can write in *kanji*. Copy the entire sentence, substituting the known *kanji*. The number of known *kanji* in each sentence is given in brackets following the sentence. Also check the textbook, かんじノート sections of Lessons 7-9, 13, 14, 17, 18, 20, and 27.

1. なかがわさんは ちいさい だいがくに いきました。[5]
　　　　川

2. あの こうこうの なかは きれい ですよ。[3]

3. きょう がっこうで なにを しましたか。[5]

4. おたんじょうびは なんがつ なんにち ですか。[5]

5. ニュースを みましたか。[1]

❺ More writing practice
If you need additional practice, trace the sample *kanji* on the previous pages, and then use blank writing practice sheets.

LESSON 36
Expressing Needs

PART 1

1. Read all of the notes for Lesson 36.

2. Learn the new vocabulary.

3. Complete Writing Practice ❷ Study, trace and write.

PART 2

1. Complete the remainder of the Writing Practice.

2. Preview the vocabulary and notes for Lesson 37.

WRITING PRACTICE

❶ Dore desu-ka? 月 日 木 本 人 大 小 何 今 火 水 金 土 見 行 学 校 中 高 年
Below each underlined part write the corresponding *kanji*. Use the correct stroke order. Check your answers by finding the words in the textbook, かんじノート sections of Lessons 7-9, 13, 14, 17, 18, 20, and 27.

1. nen	4. mite-imasu	7. takaku-nai	10. furansu-jin
2. gakkoo	5. ikanai	8. nan-nen	11. nan-bon
3. naka-ni	6. o-kane	9. kongetsu	12. moku-yoobi

❷ **Study, trace and write.**

NEN; toshi (year)

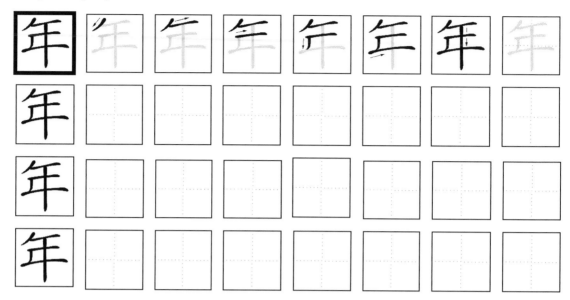

❸ **Kakimashoo!** 月 日 木 本 人 大 小 何 今 火 水 金 土 見 行 学 校 中 高 年
Read each of the following words aloud. Then underline the part(s) which you can write in *kanji*. Rewrite the entire word, substituting the known *kanji*. Use the correct stroke order. All of these words appear in section ❶.

1. おかね

2. こんげつ

3. いかない

4. がっこう

5. みています

6. ねん

7. なんぼん

8. フランスじん

9. たかくない

10. なんねん

11. もくようび

12. なかに

❹ **Dekimasu-ka?**
Read each of the following sentences aloud. Underline the part(s) which you can write in *kanji*. Copy the entire sentence, substituting the known *kanji*. The number of known *kanji* in each sentence is given in brackets following the sentence. Also check the textbook, かんじノート sections of Lessons 7-9, 13, 14, 17, 18, 20, 27 and 29.

1. こんげつ ちゅうがっこうの ともだちが ふたり にほんに いきます。[9]

二

2. きょう デパートで こうこうの にほんごの せんせいを みました。[7]

❺ **More writing practice**
If you need additional practice, trace the sample *kanji* on the previous page, and then use blank writing practice sheets.

LESSON 37
Asking for and Giving Reasons

PART 1

1. Read all of the notes for Lesson 37.

2. Learn the new vocabulary.

3. Dekimasu-ka?

Write the following verbs in *roomaji*. Then write the corresponding plain forms in *hiragana* or in *roomaji*.

-*masu* form	*roomaji*	plain form
1. たべます		
2. します		
3. いきます		
4. よみます		
5. きます		
6. かいます		
7. のみます		
8. かきます		
9. おしえます		
10. もらいます		

> Be sure to review verbs in the textbook, Interactive Activities Part 1, ❷.

PART 2

1. Dooshite kimasen-ka?

Use your imagination to respond to the following *dooshite* questions. Each answer should be an appropriate response to the question and should include one of the following:

plain form of adjective + *kara*   OR   plain form of verb + *kara*
(non-past or past)   (non-past)

Write your answers in *roomaji* or in Japanese (*kana* and *kanji*). Refer to the verb and adjective charts in the textbook, Interactive Activities section as needed. Read the example before you begin.

1. Takayama-san-wa dooshite sono hon-o kaimashita-ka?

    Jugyoo-de tsukau-kara. OR じゅぎょうで つかうから。

2. Yamakawa-san-wa dooshite eigo-no benkyoo-o shimasu-ka?

3. Nakayama-san-wa dooshite depaato-ni ikimasu-ka?

4. 本田くんは どうして 学校で ねますか。

5. 上田さんは どうして パーティーに 来ませんか。

6. 山下さんは どうして クラブに はいりませんか。

2. Preview the vocabulary and notes for Lesson 38.

LESSON 38
Locating Items in a Department Store

PART 1
---

1. Read all of the notes for Lesson 38.

2. Learn the new vocabulary.

3. Dekimasu-ka?

Write the plain past form for each of the following verbs. Remember that the plain past form is exactly like the *-te* form except that the *-te/-de* is changed to *-ta*. If you write your answers in *roomaji*, check your work by finding the correct forms in the textbook, 文法ポイント section of this lesson..

1. wasureru	wasureta OR わすれた	9. miseru	
2. iku		10. kau	
3. suru		11. kaku	
4. miru		12. kuru	
5. hanasu		13. au	
6. morau		14. tsukuru	
7. taberu		15. tsukau	
8. nomu		16. yomu	

PART 2
---

1. Yomimashoo!

This assignment provides you with an opportunity to review the *kanji* which you have learned to read. For each Japanese word or phrase, write the reading in *roomaji*.

かなと かんじ ローマじ	かなと かんじ ローマじ
1. 何の本	12. 来ません
2. 火よう日	13. 元気
3. お金	14. 小さい小学校
4. 今	15. 見ます
5. 天気	16. 今月
6. 水	17. 金よう日
7. 私	18. 何人
8. 何月何日	19. 行きました
9. 水よう日	20. 土よう日
10. 今日	21. 来年
11. 六十円	22. 上田さんと山下さん

2. Preview the vocabulary and notes for Lesson 39.

LESSON 39
Past Experiences

PART 1

1. Read all of the notes for Lesson 39.

2. Learn the new vocabulary.

3. Complete Writing Practice ❶ Study, trace and write.

PART 2

1. Complete the remainder of the Writing Practice.

2. Preview the vocabulary and notes for Lesson 40.

WRITING PRACTICE

❶ Study, trace and write.

EN (yen, circle)

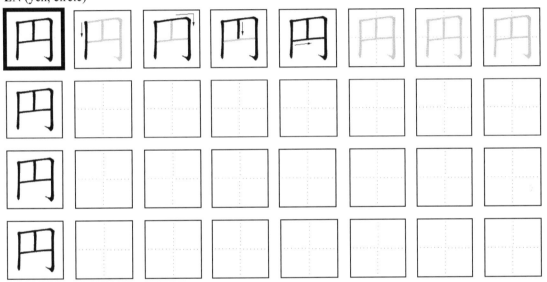

❷ **Dore desu-ka?** 月 日 木 本 人 大 小 何 今 火 水 金 土 見 行 学 校 中 高 年 円
Below each underlined part write the corresponding *kanji*. Use the correct stroke order. Check your answers by
finding the words in the textbook, かんじノート sections of Lessons 7-9, 13, 14, 17, 18, 20, 27 and 38.

1. <u>taka</u>i

2. <u>i</u>kitai

3. <u>en</u>

4. <u>kookoo</u>

5. <u>chuugaku</u>sei

6. <u>mi</u>masen deshita

7. <u>nan-nen</u>-sei

8. <u>ookiku</u>-nai

9. <u>nihonjin</u>

10. <u>kon-getsu</u>

11. <u>kin</u>-yoo<u>bi</u>

12. o-<u>mizu</u>

55

❸ **Kakimashoo!** 月 日 木 本 人 大 小 何 今 火 水 金 土 見 行 学 校 中 高 年 円
Read each of the following words aloud. Then underline the part(s) which you can write in *kanji*. Rewrite the entire word, substituting the known *kanji*. Use the correct stroke order. All of these words appear in section ❷.

1. みません でした   4. なんねんせい   7. いきたい   10. おおきくない

2. きんようび   5. たかい   8. おみず   11. こうこう

3. にほんじん   6. えん   9. こんげつ   12. ちゅうがくせい

❹ **Dekimasu-ka?**
Read each of the following sentences aloud. Underline the part(s) which you can write in *kanji*. Copy the entire sentence, substituting the known *kanji*. The number of known *kanji* in each sentence is given in brackets following the sentence. Also check the textbook, かんじノート sections of Lessons 7-9, 13, 14, 17, 18, 20, 27, 29, and 38.

1. こんげつの 15 にちに ともだちの うちで にほんの えいがを みました。[6]

2. らいねんの 8 がつ 30 にちに にほんに いって だいがくに はいって

にほんごの べんきょうを します。[11]

❺ **More writing practice**
If you need additional practice, trace the sample *kanji* on the previous page, and then use blank writing practice sheets.

LESSON 40
Review

PART 1
---

1. Read all of the notes for Lesson 40.

2. Nyuu-yooku-ni itta-koto-ga arimasu.
Write six sentences about past experiences you have had using the pattern:

. . . plain past verb + *koto-ga arimasu.* | See the textbook, Lesson 38, 文法ポイント for a list of plain past verbs. |

Three of the sentences are true, and three of them are false. Do not indicate whether the sentences are true or false, and be sure to mix them up. For your false sentences, select experiences which a クラスメート might think you actually have had since you will be trying to fool your クラスメート in the next class. If you say, for example, that you have been to the moon, your クラスメート will not have much of a challenge.

1. _____

2. _____

3. _____

4. _____

5. _____

6. _____

1. Dooshite ikimasen-ka?

Write an answer for each *dooshite* question. In the answer use the plain form of an adjective or verb followed by *kara*. Do not include the information from the question in the answer. Refer back to the textbook, Lesson 37 as needed, but DO NOT copy any answers from there. Look at the example.

Ex. どうして 行きませんか。 テレビを 見たいから。

1. どうして 行きませんか。

2. どうして その 日本ごの本を かいましたか。

3. どうして ふゆやすみに ハワイに 行きますか。

2. Dekimasu-ka?

In each line below, underline the word which does not belong. Look carefully at the meanings and the grammar. Write your reason for excluding each word in the space to the right of the line. Look at the example.

Ex.	nagai	chiisai	yasui	tokei	not an adjective
1.	ひとつ	いつ	ななつ	いつつ	
2.	あまい	からい	おいしい	たかい	
3.	かった	のんだ	わすれた	もらいました	
4.	いち	に	を	で	
5.	か	ね	よ	が	
6.	はは	あに	おとうと	おとうさん	
7.	おもしろい	しずか	うるさい	あたらしい	
8.	ゆき	あめ	はれ	あね	
9.	やすみ	ふゆ	なつ	はる	
10.	しんぶん	ほん	にん	まい	

3. Preview the vocabulary and notes for Lesson 41.

LESSON 41
Parts of the Body

1. Read all of the notes for Lesson 41.

2. Learn the new vocabulary.

3. Dekimasu-ka?

In the textbook, Interactive Activities Part 2, ❶, write each price in Arabic numerals. For example, for number 1, you would write the price ¥71,600.

1. Kakimashoo!

Carefully read the following description of a T32X—an alien of unknown origin. Then, based on the information provided, sketch the T32X. There may be many correct interpretations.

T32X

T32X-wa anmari takaku-nai desu. San-inchi-gurai desu. Karada*-wa chiisai desu. Atama-wa ookii desu. Ashi-ga yon-hon arimasu. Te-ga ni-hon arimasu. Hana-wa hitotsu arimasu. Nagai desu. Kao-no mannaka** desu. Mimi-ga mittsu arimasu. Mimi-wa atama-no ue-ni arimasu. Me-ga yottsu arimasu. Totemo chiisai desu. Mittsu-no me-wa hana-no migi de, hitotsu-no me-wa hana-no hidari desu. Kuchi-wa arimasen.

  * body   ** middle, center

2. Preview the vocabulary and notes for Lesson 42.

LESSON 42
Asking about and Describing Health Conditions

PART 1

---

1. Read all of the notes for Lesson 42.

2. Learn the new vocabulary.

3. Kanji review

Complete the following chart. Write in *roomaji* one word which (when written in Japanese) includes the given *kanji*. Underline the part of the word which would be written with that *kanji*. Then write the meaning of the word, as in the examples. You may need to refer back to Lessons 7 through 41 to check your work.

	kanji	reading	meaning		kanji	reading	meaning
1	私	<u>watashi</u>	I	13	火		
2	一月	ichi-<u>gatsu</u>	January	14	下		
3	天気	<u>ten</u>ki	weather	15	百		
4	木			16	上		
5	本			17	見		
6	人			18	大		
7	十			19	円		
8	一			20	八		
9	学			21	元		
10	何			22	万		
11	水			23	六		
12	千			24	行		

	kanji	reading	meaning		kanji	reading	meaning
25	九			35	五		
26	四			36	金		
27	七			37	来		
28	山			38	二		
29	田			39	今		
30	小			40	中		
31	高			41	年		
32	三			42	気		
33	川			43	土		
34	校			44	日		

PART 2

1. Kakimashoo!

Write the Japanese equivalent (in *kana/kanji*) for each of the following. Then check your work by finding the answers in the textbook, Interactive Activities Part 1, ❷.

1. Hello? (on the phone) _____

2. Good morning. _____

3. Where are you now? _____

4. I'm at home. _____

5. What's wrong? _____

6. I have a toothache. _____

7. Take care of yourself. _____

2. Preview the vocabulary and notes for Lesson 43.

LESSON 43
Asking about and Describing Health Conditions

PART 1

1. Read all of the notes for Lesson 43.

2. Learn the new vocabulary.

3. Kanji review

Practice writing the following *kanji* by reviewing Writing Practice ❶ in the lessons given below. With your pencil trace each *kanji* carefully, noting the correct stroke order. Then write each *kanji* at least three times on blank writing practice sheets.

学、校 (Lesson 34)   中、高 (Lesson 35)   年 (Lesson 36)   円 (Lesson 39)

4. Kakimashoo!

Read each of the following words aloud, and then write it, substituting the *kanji* which you have learned to write. Some of the words can be written entirely in *kanji*. Other words will include *hiragana* because they are normally written with *okurigana* or because you have not yet learned to write the corresponding *kanji*.

59

1. なか	6. いきました	11. らいねん
2. こうこう	7. みません	12. ちゅうがくせい
3. えん	8. すいようび	13. がっこう
4. いちねんせい	9. たかい	14. おおきくない
5. なんにち	10. しょうがっこう	15. こんげつ

1. Kyoo-no nikki (Today's journal entry)

Read the sample journal entry carefully. Then write your own imaginary journal entry, following the same pattern but using your own (1) date/day/weather notation, (2) activity, (3) description of the activity, and (4) resulting medical problem.

> ４月１８日　　　　火よう日　　　　天気：あめ
>
> 今日、一日中＊クッキーと ケーキを たべました。とても
>
> おいしかったです。でも、今、おなかが いたいから
>
> あした クッキーと ケーキは たべません。
>
> ＊一日中 = ichi-nichi-juu = all day

---

2. Preview the vocabulary and notes for Lesson 44.

LESSON 44
Taking Medicine

1. Read all of the notes for Lesson 44.

2. Learn the new vocabulary.

3. Time line

On the personal time line that follows are a number of events (*asa-gohan, jugyoo, miitingu, deeto*, etc.) which occurred during one day. Use your imagination as you complete the time line by writing what you did before (*-no mae-ni*) OR after (*-no ato-de*) each event. Write a different activity on each line. Be sure to use the past tense (*-mashita*). Look at the examples.

ASA-GOHAN
Asa-gohan-*no ato-de* (OR Jugyoo-*no mae-ni*) nihongo-no benkyoo-o shimashita.

JUGYOO

HIRU-GOHAN

MIITINGU

TENISU-NO SHIAI

BAN-GOHAN

DEETO
Deeto-*no ato-de* uchi-ni kaette, terebi-o mite, nemashita.

PART 2

1. Dekimasu-ka?

In each line below, underline the word which does not belong. Look carefully at the meanings and the grammar. Write your reason for excluding each word in the space to the right of the line. Look at the example.

Ex.	nagai	chiisai	yasui	<u>tokei</u>	not an adjective

1. あし　　あした　　あたま　　のど

2. 目　　耳　　日　　口

3. て　　はな　　みみ　　め

4. くすり　　がっこう　　いしゃ　　びょういん

5. まえに　　はちじに　　あとで　　なに

6. かぜ　　せんせい　　じゅぎょう　　べんきょう

7. 行きます　　見ます　　来ます　　です

8. ゆき　　あめ　　はれ　　あね

9. 水　　火　　本　　木

10. 年　　万　　月　　日

2. Non-stop talking

Complete three one-minute rounds. During each round say as much as you can about ailments and taking medicine. Remember that if you draw a blank, just keep repeating the same sentence or phrase until you can continue. Try to avoid pauses.

3. Preview the vocabulary and notes for Lesson 45.

LESSON 45
Describing People (Personality)

PART 1
---

1. Read all of the notes for Lesson 45.

2. Learn the new vocabulary.

3. Kakimashoo!
For each set of words below write one complete sentence in Japanese (*kana/kanji*). Use the words in the order given and add the needed particles (*-wa*, *-no*, etc.) to create grammatically correct sentences. If you wish, you may add other words to make your sentences more interesting. Be sure to change the first adjective to the linking *-te* form. Look at the examples carefully before you begin.

1. Honda / majime / kibishii

   本田せんせいはまじめできびしいです。

2. Sono eiga / takai / tsumaranai

   そのえいがは高くてつまらないです。

3. Kono keeki / yasui / oishii

4. Tanaka / konpyuutaa / atarashii / hayai

   田

5. Ano sensei / yasashii / omoshiroi

6. Akiko / shizuka / majime

7. Takada / jugyoo / nagai / tsumaranai

   田

PART 2
---

1. Kakimashoo!
Read the sample description of a teacher. Then write your own description of an <u>imaginary</u> teacher, following the same pattern but changing (1) the school subject, (2) the teacher's name, (3) the age, and (4) the two adjectives describing the teacher. You may also wish to change the last sentence. Write in Japanese, including any *kanji* which you have learned to write. If you have successfully completed the Optional Writing Practices, you may also include any of those *kanji*.

私のえいごのせんせいはスミスせんせいです。スミスせんせいは４０才ぐらいです。元気であかるいです。私はスミスせんせいが大すきです。

単語

すう学	れきし	ドイツご	フランスご
ちり	スペインご	日本ご	たいいく
すき	すきじゃない	あんまり すきじゃない	

2. Preview the vocabulary and notes for Lesson 46.

LESSON 46
Describing People (Physical Characteristics)

PART 1

1. Read all of the notes for Lesson 46.

2. Learn the new vocabulary.

3. Complete Writing Practice ❶ Study, trace and write.

PART 2

1. Complete the remainder of the Writing Practice.

2. Preview the vocabulary and notes for Lesson 47.

WRITING PRACTICE

❶ **Study, trace and write.**

SAI (talent; *suffix for counting age*)

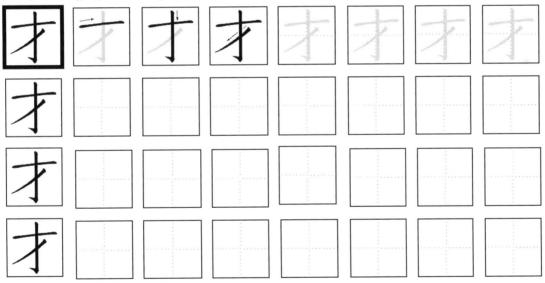

❷ **Dore desu-ka?** 月 日 木 本 人 大 小 何 今 火 水 金 土 見 行 学 校 中 高 年 円 才
Below each underlined part write the corresponding *kanji*. Use the correct stroke order. Check your answers by finding the words in the textbook, かんじノート sections of Lessons 7-9, 13, 14, 17, 18, 20, 27, 29, 38, and 45.

1. <u>nan</u>-<u>nen</u>	4. <u>chuugakkoo</u> [3 *kanji*]	7. <u>takaku</u>-te	10. <u>Nihon-Daigaku</u>
2. <u>kotoshi</u> [2 *kanji*]	5. <u>nan</u>-<u>sai</u>	8. <u>i</u>kitaku-nai	11. <u>do</u>-yoobi
3. <u>mi</u>tai	6. 100-<u>en</u>	9. <u>kyoo</u> [2 *kanji*]	12. 15-<u>sai</u>

❸ **Kakimashoo!** 月 日 木 本 人 大 小 何 今 火 水 金 土 見 行 学 校 中 高 年 円 才
Read each of the following words aloud. Then underline the part(s) which you can write in *kanji*. Rewrite the entire word, substituting the known *kanji*. Use the correct stroke order. All of these words appear in section ❷.

1. ちゅうがっこう　　4. きょう　　　　7. にほん だいがく　10. たかくて

2. どようび　　　　　5. なんねん　　　8. 十五さい　　　　11. ことし

3. なんさい　　　　　6. いきたくない　9. みたい　　　　　12. 百えん

❹ **Dekimasu-ka?**
Read each of the following sentences aloud. Underline the part(s) which you can write in *kanji*. Copy the entire sentence, substituting the known *kanji*. The number of known *kanji* in each sentence is given in brackets following the sentence. Also check the textbook, かんじノート sections of Lessons 7-9, 13, 14, 17, 18, 20, 27, 29, 38, and 45.

1. おたんじょうびは なんがつ なんにち ですか。[5]

2. ことし なんさいに なりますか。[4]

3. いま こうこう なんねんせい ですか。[5]

❺ **More writing practice**
If you need additional practice, trace the sample *kanji* on the previous page, and then use blank writing practice sheets.

LESSON 47
Describing People (Clothing)

PART 1
---

1. Read all of the notes for Lesson 47.

2. Learn the new vocabulary.

3. Change the dialogue.
Create a new version of the dialogue in the textbook, Interactive Activities Part 1, ❷ by replacing the missing words with your own choice of descriptive words. You may make the thief a man or a woman. Write in *kana/kanji*.

B: (looking in dismay at the bananas, sees the policeman approaching) あ、おまわりさん！
(gestures to come) こっちです。
A: どうしたんですか。
B: (upset) どろぼうです。見てください。　(points to the bananas)
A: (shakes head) ああ、どろぼうを 見ましたか。
B: はい、見ました。
A: (pulls out pad and pen, starts taking notes) どんな人でしたか。
B: _____ でした。(shows approximate height with hand)
A: (writing) _____。
B: それから、かみが _____ です。
A: (writing) かみが _____んですね。
B: (nodding) はい。
A: 何才ぐらい でしたか。

B: (thinks hard) ええと、＿＿＿＿＿＿＿＿＿＿＿＿＿＿ でした。

Now complete this one-line extension of the dialogue.

B: それから、＿＿＿＿＿＿＿＿＿＿＿＿ の人 でした。

↑

Describe the thief by including one color word (see COLORS box in the textbook, Interactive Activities Part 2, ❷) + an item of clothing.

PART 2
---

1. Yomimashoo!

Read each of the following sentences aloud, and then write the <u>one</u> correct reading for each *kanji* below it. Write the readings of the *kanji* in *hiragana*. Look at the example.

Ex. 上から二ばん目の本を下さい。
　　うえ　　に　　　め　ほん　くだ

1. 私の 高校は あんまり大きくない です。

2. あの人は 中学校の 先生です。

3. ともだちの 名前は 山川くんです。

4. 今年の 三月に 田中さんは 二十五オに なります。

5. 金よう日の 天気は よかったです。

6. 高田さんから 何を もらいましたか。

7. さいふの 中に お金が 九万八千六百七十円 あります。

2. Preview the vocabulary and notes for Lesson 48.

LESSON 48
Knowing People and Things

PART 1
---

1. Read all of the notes for Lesson 48.

2. Learn the new vocabulary.

3. Complete Writing Practice ❶ Study, trace and write.

PART 2
---

1. Complete the remainder of the Writing Practice.

2. Preview the vocabulary and notes for Lesson 49.

WRITING PRACTICE

❶ Study, trace and write.

SEN; saki* (previous, ahead)

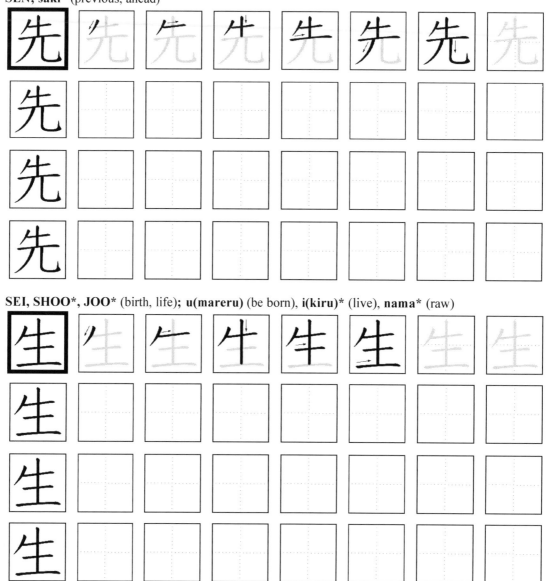

SEI, SHOO*, JOO* (birth, life); **u(mareru)** (be born), **i(kiru)*** (live), **nama*** (raw)

❷ Dore desu-ka? 月 日 木 本 人 大 小 山 川 何 今 火 水 金 土 見 行 学 校 中 高 年 円 才 先 生
Below each underlined part write the corresponding *kanji*. Use the correct stroke order. Check your answers by finding the words in the textbook, かんじノート sections of Lessons 7-9, 13, 14, 17, 18, 20, 27, 29, 38, 45 and 47.

1. <u>sen</u>getsu

2. nan-<u>sai</u>

3. 1200-<u>en</u>

4. <u>daigaku</u>

5. <u>mi</u>taku-nai

6. <u>kyoo</u> [2 *kanji*]

7. <u>kongetsu</u>

8. <u>kin-yoobi</u>

9. 59-<u>sai</u>

10. <u>sensei</u>

11. <u>takakatta</u>

12. <u>chuugakusei</u>

| 13. <u>oo</u>kiku-nai | 15. <u>gakkoo</u>-no <u>naka</u> | 17. <u>Nihon</u> | 19. <u>ka</u>-yoo<u>bi</u> |
| 14. <u>iki</u>masen | 16. o-<u>mizu</u> | 18. o-<u>kane</u> | 20. <u>nan</u>-<u>nin</u> |

❸ **Kakimashoo!** 月 日 木 本 人 大 小 山 川 何 今 火 水 金 土 見 行 学 校 中 高 年 円 才 先 生
Read each of the following words aloud. Then underline the part(s) which you can write in *kanji*. Rewrite the entire word, substituting the known *kanji*. Use the correct stroke order. All of these words appear in section ❷.

1. おかね	6. みたくない	11. 五十九さい	16. にほん
2. こんげつ	7. たかかった	12. だいがく	17. きょう
3. おおきくない	8. がっこうのなか	13. ちゅうがくせい	18. いきません
4. せんせい	9. おみず	14. なんにん	19. 千二百えん
5. かようび	10. せんげつ	15. きんようび	20. なんさい

❹ **Dekimasu-ka?**
Read each of the following sentences aloud. Underline the part(s) which you can write in *kanji*. Copy the entire sentence, substituting the known *kanji*. The number of known *kanji* in each sentence is given in brackets following the sentence. Also check the textbook, かんじノート sections of Lessons 7-9, 13, 14, 17, 18, 20, 27, 29, 38, 45 and 47.

1. だいがくの せんせいは どこで にほんごの べんきょうを しましたか。 [6]

2. ことしの １０がつに なんさいに なりますか。 [5]

3. にほんの えいがを みたことが ありますか。 [3]

4. その ちいさい ほんは とても たかかった です。 [3]

❺ **More writing practice**
If you need additional practice, trace the sample *kanji* on the previous page, and then use blank writing practice sheets.

LESSON 49
Life Events (Birth and Marriage)

PART 1
---

1. Read all of the notes for Lesson 49.

2. Learn the vocabulary.

3. Kakimashoo!
Read the sample journal entry carefully. Then write your own imaginary journal entry, following the same pattern but using your own ideas for the (1) date/day/weather notation, (2) person's name, (3) birth information, (4) marriage information, (5) number of children, and (6) person's personality. Include only those *kanji* which you have learned how to write. Proof and edit your work.

5月10日　木よう日　　　　　　　　天気：はれ

　今日、とても おもしろい 人に あいました。名前は 田中さん です。田中さんは とうきょうで うまれました。今年、七十八才に なります。けっこんしていて、こどもさんが 六人います。田中さんは あかるくて 元気な 人 です。

PART 2

1. Kakimashoo!

Rewrite your journal entry (Part 1, 2. Kakimashoo!), incorporating the corrections which you made during the textbook, Interactive Activities Part 2, ❶. When you have finished writing, read the journal entry aloud twice.

2. Preview the vocabulary and notes for Lesson 50.

LESSON 50
Where People Live

PART 1

1. Read all of the notes for Lesson 50.

2. Learn the new vocabulary.

3. Dore desu-ka? 月 日 木 本 人 大 小 何 今 火 水 金 土 見 行 学 校 中 高 年 円 才 先 生
Below each underlined part write the corresponding *kanji*. Use the correct stroke order. Write everything else in *hiragana*. After you have completely finished, check your answers by finding the words (in mixed order) in the box that follows.

1. <u>gakusei</u>

2. <u>oo</u>kiku-<u>nakatta</u>

3. <u>ima</u>

4. o-<u>kane</u>

5. <u>chii</u>saku-nai

6. san-<u>gatsu</u>

7. kyuu-<u>sai</u>

8. o-<u>mizu</u>

9. <u>shoogakusei</u>

10. hyaku-<u>en</u>

11. <u>nan</u>-<u>nichi</u>

12. <u>kotoshi</u>

13. <u>chuugoku</u>-<u>jin</u>

14. <u>mi</u>masen deshita

15. <u>sui</u>-<u>yoobi</u>

16. <u>kookoosei</u>

17. <u>konshuu</u>

18. <u>sensei</u>

19. <u>ikanai</u>

20. <u>nan</u>-<u>nen</u>-<u>sei</u>

小学生	今しゅう	小さくない	先生
お金	今年	きゅうオ	お水
中ごく人	行かない	今	何年生
ひゃく円	学生	高校生	大きくなかった
さん月	水よう日	何日	見ませんでした

PART 2

1. Kakimashoo!
Read each of the following words aloud. Then underline the part(s) which you can write in *kanji*. Rewrite the entire word, substituting the known *kanji*. Use the correct stroke order. All of these words appear in Part 1, 2. Dore desu-ka?.

1. すいようび

2. さんがつ

3. がくせい

4. きゅうさい

5. ちゅうごくじん

6. おみず

7. ひゃくえん

8. おおきくなかった

9. なんねんせい

10. いかない

11. せんせい

12. こんしゅう

13. ことし

14. なんにち

15. こうこうせい

16. おかね

17. しょうがくせい

18. ちいさくない

19. いま

20. みませんでした

2. Dekimasu-ka?
Each of the following sentences is written with no spaces between the words. Rewrite each sentence entirely, substituting the number of known *kanji* shown in brackets.

1. こうこう の にほんご の せんせい は やさしい ですか。 [6]

2. いま ちゅうがく なんねんせい ですか。 [6]

3. Preview the vocabulary and notes for Lesson 51.

69

LESSON 51
Relatives

1. Read all of the notes for Lesson 51.

2. Learn the new vocabulary.

3. Kakimashoo!

Using the completed Tanaka family tree in the textbook, Interactive Activities Part 1, ❷, write three true statements and three false statements about the Tanaka family. Write in *kana/kanji*. Mix the true and false statements since in the next class you will be challenging a クラスメート with a short listening exercise. You may wish to jot down an answer key on another page. Before you begin writing your sentences, read these examples, check the tree, and mark each as true or false.

Ex. 1. ともこさんはけんじさんとけっこんしています。
Ex. 2. ゆきおくんのおかあさんは３３才です。

1. _____
2. _____
3. _____
4. _____
5. _____
6. _____

PART 2

1. Yomimashoo!

This assignment provides you with an opportunity to review the *kanji* which you have learned to read. For each Japanese word, phrase, or sentence, write the reading in *roomaji*. Then write the meaning in English.

	かなとかんじ	ローマじ	えいご
1	何の本		
2	火よう日の 前の日		
3	子ども		
4	高い山		
5	今日の 天気		
6	三才に なりました。		
7	私は水を のみました。		
8	何月何日		
9	小さい小学校		
10	父と母		
11	一万三千四百六十円		
12	山下さんは 来ません。		
13	元気 じゃない です。		
14	見ます		
15	山下くんが 行った。		
16	来年の 先生		

2. Preview the vocabulary and notes for Lesson 52.

LESSON 52
Occupations

PART 1

1. Read all of the notes for Lesson 52.

2. Learn the new vocabulary.

3. Kakimashoo!
Write a short description of one of Masayo's relatives who appears in the completed chart in the textbook, Interactive Activities Part 1, ❷. Write in Japanese, including any *kanji* which you have learned to write. If you have successfully completed the Optional Writing Practices, you may also include any of those *kanji*. **Include** (1) the person's relationship to Masayo, (2) the person's name [Use your imagination.], (3) occupation, (4) place of work, and (5) work hours. Use your imagination to **include at least three** additional pieces of information such as physical description, age, personality, daily routine, transportation to work, description of the work, or description of the place of work. Read the example carefully and use it as a guide. Do not write about Masayo's *ojiisan*.

まさよさんの おじいさんの 名前は 中川たけしさん です。六十五才です。
がかです。うちで はたらいています。まい日 おそく*おきて、あさごはん
を たべて、十じから 四じまで しごとを します。　　　　　　＊ late

PART 2

1. Kanji review
Practice writing the following *kanji* by reviewing Writing Practice ❶ in the lessons given below. With your pencil trace each *kanji* carefully, noting the correct stroke order. Then write each *kanji* at least three times on blank writing practice sheets.

才 (Lesson 46)　　　　先、生 (Lesson 48)

2. Kakimashoo!
Read each of the following words aloud, and then write it, substituting the *kanji* which you have learned to write. Some of the words can be written entirely in *kanji*. Other words will include *hiragana* because they are normally written with *okurigana* or because you have not yet learned to write the corresponding *kanji*.

1. たかい	6. せんせい	11. おかね
2. こうこう	7. みません	12. しょうがくせい
3. えん	8. なか	13. いきました
4. ことし	9. せんげつ	14. 三十四さい
5. なんねん	10. ちゅうがっこう	15. いま

3. Preview the vocabulary and notes for Lesson 53.

LESSON 53
Getting a Job

PART 1

1. Read all of the notes for Lesson 53.

2. Learn the new vocabulary.

3. Rirekisho (Résumé)

The simplified résumé here has many of the same sections that you would find on the standard Japanese *rirekisho* form which you see in the video. Complete the résumé in Japanese (wherever possible) using *roomaji* or *kana/kanji*. You will be using this résumé in the textbook, Interactive Activities Part 2, ❶ as you are interviewed for a summer job. You may use your imagination for part or all of the résumé. You may wish to create a résumé which is rather unique. For example, maybe you are a 高校三年生 , but you are 十五才. Possibly, 日本ごとフランスごと中ごくごができます。

Which job are you applying for? _____

名前		男　・　女
年　　　　　月　　　　　日生 [birthdate]		才 [age]
じゅうしょ 住所	でんわばんごう 電話番号 （　　　　）	
れんらくさき 連絡先 [contact person]	でんわばんごう 電話番号 （　　　　）	

Now provide a list of the schools you have attended (elementary, middle, etc.). On the first line write *Name of school* 小学校 and give the year and month you entered the school. On the next line write the name of your elementary school again, this time giving the year and month you graduated or transferred. Do the same for other schools you have attended. For your current school, make only one entry. Also list here any work experience you have had, giving both beginning and ending dates.

年	月	がくれき　しょくれき 学歴・職歴　[Educational and Work History]

Now provide a list of your licenses, certificates, and qualifications. For students, this is the section in which you will want to list your abilities and skills (*kuruma-no unten*, languages you can speak, etc.) If you had a course or special training (for example, first aid) or were awarded a certificate or license (for example, a driving license), you will want to give the year and month.

年	月	めんきょしゅうとくしかく 免許・習得・資格　[Licenses, Certificates, and Qualifications]

Now fill out the following section which includes your favorite subjects, hobbies, sports, and state of health. "Motivation for choice" means why do you want this job for which you are applying.

とくい　がっか 得意な学科 [Strong Subject]	けんこうじょうたい 健康状態 [State of Health]
しゅみ 趣味	しぼう　どうき 志望の動機 [Motivation for Choice]
スポーツ	

Finally, you need to provide some information on your immediate family: names, their relationships to you, and their ages.

	名前	せいべつ 性別　[Sex]	ねんれい 年令　[Age]
か ぞ く			

PART 2

1. Yomimashoo!

This assignment provides you with an opportunity to review the *kanji* which you have learned to read. For each Japanese word, phrase, or sentence, write the reading in *roomaji*. Then write the meaning in English.

	かなとかんじ	ローマじ	えいご
1	お名前は？		
2	大学生です。		
3	今、テレビを見ている。		
4	もう一ど言ってください。		
5	今日の天気		
6	十七才		
7	でん話といいます。		
8	行きませんでした。		
9	小さい小学校		
10	お父さんとお母さん		
11	話します		
12	山下先生		
13	お元気ですか。		
14	上田くんが来ます。		

2. Preview the vocabulary and notes for Lesson 54.

LESSON 54
After Graduation

PART 1

1. Read all of the notes for Lesson 54.

2. Learn the new vocabulary.

3. Kakimashoo!

Write a description of one of the university students who appears in the completed chart in the textbook,

Interactive Activities Part 1, ❷. Write in Japanese, including any *kanji* which you have learned to write. If you have successfully completed the Optional Writing Practices, you may also include any of those *kanji*. **Include** (1) the student's name, (2) his/her year at the university (not shown in the chart), (3) when he/she will graduate, (4) what he/she will do after graduation, and (5) where he/she will work. **Also include at least three** additional pieces of information such as (but not limited to) physical description, personality, age, work, description of the work place, or why he/she wants to do that work. Read the example carefully and use it as a guide. Do not write about Watanabe-san. Continue your description on the next page if you need more space.

わたなべさんは 今、大学二年生 です。あたまが いい人です。まい日としょかんで 五じかんぐらいべんきょう します。わたなべさんは 二年ごにそつぎょうします。そのあと、目いしゃに なります。大学びょういんではたらきます。

Can you answer these questions (orally) about the description you just wrote?

1. いつ 大学を そつぎょうしますか。

2. その あと、何を しますか。

3. どこで はたらきますか。

PART 2

1. Yomimashoo!
This assignment provides you with an opportunity to review the *kanji* which you have recently learned to read. For each Japanese word, phrase, or sentence, write the reading in *roomaji*. Then write the meaning in English.

	かなとかんじ	ローマじ	えいご
1	国		
2	話します		
3	日本語		
4	中国		
5	言いました		
6	何語		
7	でん話		

	かなとかんじ	ローマじ	えいご
8	父と母		
9	目		
10	山口先生		
11	お父さんの名前		
12	九百		
13	耳		
14	がい来語		
15	先月の天気		
16	来年の先生		

2. Preview the vocabulary and notes for Lesson 55.

LESSON 55
Dreams for the Future

PART 1
---

1. Read all of the notes for Lesson 55.

2. Learn the new vocabulary.

3. Kakimashoo!
Use your imagination and assume the identity of one of the people who appears in the chart in the textbook Interactive Activities Part 1, ❷. Write about your imaginary self in Japanese, including any *kanji* which you have learned to write. If you have successfully completed the Optional Writing Practices, you may also include any of those *kanji*. **Include** (1) your name, (2) what you wanted to become (when you were a child), (3) what you now want to become, (4) whether you want to get married, (5) whether you want to have children and how many, and (6) where you want to live in the future. Use your imagination to **include at least three** additional pieces of information. Read the example carefully and use it as a guide. Do <u>not</u> choose *Joonzu*.

私の 名前は ジョーンズです。今、高校三年生 です。子どもの とき 先生に
なりたかった です。でも、今、いしゃに なりたい です。しょう来、やさしくて
あたまが いい人と けっこん したい です。子どもが 一人ほしい です。おんな
の子が ほしい です。モンタナに すみたい です。小さくて しずかな まちに
すみたい です。

_____

_____

_____

_____

_____

_____

1. Kakimashoo!
Write about your dreams for the future in Japanese, including any *kanji* which you have learned to write. If you have successfully completed the Optional Writing Practices, you may also include any of those *kanji* **Include** (1) your name, (2) what you wanted to become (when you were a child), (3) what you now want to become, (4) whether you want to get married or not, (5) whether you want to have children and how many, and (6) where you want to live in the future. **Include at least three** additional pieces of information. Use the sample on the previous page as a guide.

_____

_____

_____

_____

_____

_____

_____

_____

2. Preview the vocabulary and notes for Lesson 56.

LESSON 56
Review

PART 1

1. Read all of the notes for Lesson 56.

2. Kakimashoo!
Read the sample journal entry carefully. Then write your own imaginary journal entry, following the same pattern but using your own ideas for the (1) date/day/weather notation, (2) person's name, (3) birth information, (4) places the person lived at different times in his/her life, (5) marriage information, (6) number of children, and (7) the person's occupation. You may include additional information in your description. Write entirely in Japanese, including only those *kanji* which you have learned how to write. If you have successfully completed the Optional Writing Practices, you may include any of those *kanji* as well. Write your entry in the space after the journal entry.

４月２８日　　　　　金よう日　　　　　天気：あめ

今日、とても やさしくて おもしろい 人に あいました。名前は 山口としおさん です。山口さんは よこはまで 生まれました。今、五十七才です。おたんじょう 日は 三月十九日です。子どもの とき、よこはまに すんでいました。中学生の とき、おばあさんと とうきょうに すんでいました。高校生の とき、三年かん アメリカに すんでいました。そのとき、お父さんは アメリカの かいしゃで はたらいていました。大学生の とき、メキシコに 行って、スペイン語の べんきょうを しました。大学三年生の とき、あかるくて 元気な おんなの人に あいました。そつぎょうの あと、その人と けっこん しました。

今、カリフォルニアに すんでいます。子どもが 五人 います。山口さんは 高校で
スペイン語と 日本語を おしえています。

_____

_____

_____

_____

_____

_____

_____

_____

_____

_____

_____

_____

PART 2

1. Yomimashoo!

This assignment provides you with an opportunity to review the *kanji* which you have recently learned to read. For each Japanese word or phrase, write the reading in *roomaji*. Then write the meaning in English. Check your answers by finding the words in mixed order in the list of words that follow.

	かなとかんじ	ローマじ		かなとかんじ	ローマじ
1	来年		18	土よう日	
2	火よう日		19	お金	
3	書きます		20	私	
4	今		21	読みません	
5	天気		22	八万人	
6	水		23	子ども	
7	中国語		24	何月何日	
8	言いました		25	日本語の本	
9	水よう日と 金よう日		26	上田さんと 山下さん	
10	今日		27	来ません	
11	三百六十五円		28	今年	
12	話します		29	先生	
13	元気		30	行きました	
14	何人		31	九十四才	
15	見ます		32	小さい小学校	
16	今月		33	口	
17	目と耳		34	名前	

rainen kayoobi kyoo suiyoobi-to kinyoobi hanashimasu mimasu Ueda-san-to Yamashita-san kuchi ima tenki mizu chuugokugo nan-nin doyoobi hachi-man-nin kimasen ikimashita namae iimashita san-byaku roku-juu-go-en me-to mimi watashi nan-gatsu nan-nichi sensei kyuu-juu-yon-sai genki kongetsu o-kane yomimasen kodomo nihongo-no hon kakimasu kotoshi chiisai shoogakkoo

2. Preview the vocabulary and notes for Lesson 57.

LESSON 57
Length of Events

1. Read all of the notes for Lesson 57.

2. Learn the new vocabulary.

2. Kakimashoo!

Write a short description of one of the people who appears in the completed chart in the textbook Interactive Activities Part 1, ❷. Write in Japanese, including any *kanji* which you have learned to write. If you have successfully completed the Optional Writing Practices, you may also include any of those *kanji*. **Include** (1) the person's name, (2) occupation, (3) where he/she went, (4) length of the stay, and (5) what he/she did there. Use your imagination to **include at least three** additional pieces of information. Read the example carefully and use it as a guide. Do not write about Yamaguchi.

> 山口さんは パイロット です。きょ年の あき、ごかぞくと いっしょに ハワイに 行きました。ハワイに 一しゅう間ぐらい いました。ハワイの うみで あそびました。サーフィンと スキューバダイビングを しました。おいしい パイナップルを たくさん たべました。

1. Yomimashoo!

Read each of the following passages aloud, and then answer the questions by writing in Japanese, including any *kanji* which you have learned to write. If you have successfully completed the Optional Writing Practices, you may also include any of those *kanji*.

> 私の 中国語の 先生は スミス先生 です。スミス先生は 四十才ぐらい です。元気で あかるい人 です。私は スミス先生が 大すきです。

1. 先生のお名前は何ですか。➜

2. 何才ぐらいですか。➜

3. どんな人ですか。➜

今日、とても おもしろい 人に あいました。お名前は 田中さんです。 田中さんは とうきょうで 生まれました。二十三才の とき、けっこんしました。子どもさんが 六人います。

4. 田中さんは どこで 生まれましたか。➜

5. いつ けっこんしましたか。➜

6. 子どもさんが 何人 いますか。➜

りかさんの おばあさんの お名前は 中川ちよさんです。六十五才です。がか です。うちで はたらいています。まい日 八じに おきて、あさごはんを たべて、十じから 四じまで えを かきます。ひるごはんは たべません。

7. 中川さんの おしごとは 何ですか。➜

8. 中川さんは まい日 何じ間ぐらい はたらきますか。➜

2. Preview the vocabulary and notes for Lesson 58.

LESSON 58
Travel Schedules

PART 1

1. Read all of the notes for Lesson 58.

2. Learn the new vocabulary.

3. Kakimashoo!
Write the following lengths of time in *roomaji*, then in English.

	かなとかんじ	ローマじ	えいご
1	三しゅう間		
2	一か月間		
3	二日間		
4	六か月間		
5	五年間		
6	十日間		
7	九年間		
8	三日間		
9	何年間		
10	四しゅう間		
11	十か月間		
12	二しゅう間		
13	一日		
14	四年間		
15	六しゅう間		
16	四日間		
17	二か月間		
18	一しゅう間		

1. Kakimashoo!
Read this description of part of Ikeda-san's trip. Answer the questions in Japanese, including any *kanji* which you have learned to write. If you have successfully completed the Optional Writing Practices, you may also include any of those *kanji*. Write complete sentences.

ぼくは 七月に サンフランシスコに 行きます。五日間の ツアーです。とうきょう
から サンフランシスコまで ひこうきで 行きます。ひこうきは 二十日の ごご
四時五分に でて、二十日の ごぜん 九時十分に つきます。つぎの 日、バスで
ヨセミテこうえんに 行きます。あさの 八時に でて、ひるの 十二時に つきます。
ヨセミテこうえんで きれいな 山と みずうみを 見たいです。その 日の よる、
サンフランシスコの ホテルに かえります。

1. いけださんは いつ サンフランシスコに 行きますか。➜

2. どれぐらい サンフランシスコに いますか。➜

3. (a) ひこうきは 何時に でますか。➜

   (b) ひこうきは 何時に つきますか。➜

   (c) Why do you think it is arriving at an earlier time on the same day? Can you calculate the traveling time? ➜

4. (a) いけださんは サンフランシスコから どこに 行きますか。➜

   (b) そこまで バスで 何時間ですか。➜

2. Preview the vocabulary and notes for Lesson 59.

LESSON 59
Famous Tourist Sights in Japan

1. Read all of the notes for Lesson 59.

2. Learn the new vocabulary.

3. Yomimashoo!
Read each of the following passages aloud, and then answer the questions by writing in Japanese, including any *kanji* which you have learned to write. If you have successfully completed the Optional Writing Practices, you may also include any of those *kanji*.

私は 六月二日から アルバイトを しています。大きい デパートで はたらい
ています。デパートは 私の うちに ちかい です。しごとは 火よう日から
土よう日まで です。八時から 五時まで です。一時間 九ドルです。お金が
いいから、しごとが 大すき です。

Imagine that the above is your own journal entry. How would you answer these questions?

1. どこで はたらいて いますか。 ➡

2. デパートは どこ ですか。 ➡

3. 金よう日に はたらきますか。 ➡

4. どうして しごとが すき ですか。 ➡

> クリスさんは、今、大学三年生 です。おんがくの べんきょうを して
> います。来年、そつぎょう します。その あと、中学校で おんがくを
> おしえます。

5. クリスさんは いつ そつぎょう しますか。 ➡

6. 何の かもくを おしえますか。 ➡

PART 2

1. Kakimashoo!
Use your imagination. You have just returned from the Japan trip which you planned in the textbook, Interactive Activities Part 2, ❷. Write a short description of part of your trip. **Include** (1) two consecutive destinations, (2) some arrival and departure dates, (3) length of stay, and (4) what you did. Write in Japanese (except for place names you do not know in Japanese), including any *kanji* which you have learned to write. If you have successfully completed the Optional Writing Practices, you may also include any of those *kanji*. Write in the past tense. Study the example.

> 五月三十日に <u>なら</u>*に 行きました。ご前十一時に つきました。Deer Park に
> 行って、ピクニックを しました。その あと、Todaiji Templeに 行って、
> しゃしんを たくさん とりました。ならに 二日間 いました。ならから
> おおさかまで でんしゃで 行きました。そこで 日本人の ともだちに あって、
> Osaka Castleに 行きました。おおさかに 六月四日まで いました。
>
> *Nara (a city near Kyoto)

_____

_____

_____

_____

_____

_____

_____

2. Preview the vocabulary and notes for Lesson 60.

LESSON 60
Transportation Arrangements

---

1. Read all of the notes for Lesson 60.

2. Learn the new vocabulary.

3. Kakimashoo!
Write the Japanese for each of the following, including as many *kanji* as you have learned how to write.

	えい語	日本語		えい語	日本語
1	what month and date		9	now	
2	a small book		10	a 2nd-year student	
3	I saw the money.		11	Thursday and Saturday	
4	ten years old		12	30 yen	
5	a Japanese person		13	a middle school student	
6	a big university		14	today	
7	water		15	went	
8	a high school teacher				

---

1. Dekimasu-ka?
In each line below, underline the *kanji* which does not belong. Write your reason for excluding each word in the space to the right of the line. Look at the example.

Ex.	年	月	日	<u>何</u>	not a length of time
1.	母	火	父	子	
2.	万	六	四	九	
3.	才	水	土	月	
4.	聞	駅	話	読	
5.	目	時	日	分	
6.	上	前	国	下	
7.	雨	天気	元気	雪	
8.	百	話	語	読	
9.	耳	口	日	目	

Now write <u>one</u> grammatically correct sentence in Japanese using as many of the *kanji* you have excluded above as you can. Circle the target *kanji* you have included. If you have not learned how to write some of the *kanji*, write them in *hiragana* instead. (The meaning of the sentence may be a bit unusual.)

_____

_____

2. Preview the vocabulary and notes for Lesson 61.

LESSON 61
Describing Lost Items

1. Read all of the notes for Lesson 61.

2. Learn the new vocabulary.

3. Change the dialogue.
Create a new version of the dialogue in the textbook, Interactive Activities Part 1, ❷ by replacing the missing words with your own choice of words. Write in *kana/kanji*.

山口：すみません。＿＿＿＿＿＿＿＿＿＿＿＿＿＿＿が なくなりました。
かばん・バックパック・バッグ・スーツケース

中川：すみません。(pauses) どんな ＿＿＿＿＿＿＿＿＿ですか。(picks up a pen to write)

山口：ええと、(showing size with hands) ＿＿＿＿＿＿＿＿＿＿＿＿＿＿です。

中川：＿＿＿＿＿＿＿＿＿＿＿ (writes) の 中に 何が はいっていましたか。

山口：＿＿＿＿＿＿と ＿＿＿＿＿＿＿です。

中川：＿＿＿＿＿＿と ＿＿＿＿＿＿＿！それは たいへん ですね。

1. Kakimashoo!
Write a description of an (imaginary) item you have lost. Write in Japanese, including any *kanji* which you have learned to write. If you have successfully completed the Optional Writing Practices, you may also include any of those *kanji*. **Include** (1) what the lost item is, (2) a description of the item—size, color, etc., and (3) when and where you think you lost it. You may include additional information. Read the example carefully and use it as a guide.

> 私の 日本語の 本が なくなりました。大きくて あかい本 です。 今日、
> ともだちと としょかんに 行って、日本語の べんきょうを しました。
> それから レストランに 行きました。そこに 本を わすれました。

＿＿＿＿＿＿＿＿＿＿＿＿＿＿＿＿＿＿＿＿＿＿＿＿＿＿＿＿＿＿＿＿

＿＿＿＿＿＿＿＿＿＿＿＿＿＿＿＿＿＿＿＿＿＿＿＿＿＿＿＿＿＿＿＿

＿＿＿＿＿＿＿＿＿＿＿＿＿＿＿＿＿＿＿＿＿＿＿＿＿＿＿＿＿＿＿＿

＿＿＿＿＿＿＿＿＿＿＿＿＿＿＿＿＿＿＿＿＿＿＿＿＿＿＿＿＿＿＿＿

＿＿＿＿＿＿＿＿＿＿＿＿＿＿＿＿＿＿＿＿＿＿＿＿＿＿＿＿＿＿＿＿

＿＿＿＿＿＿＿＿＿＿＿＿＿＿＿＿＿＿＿＿＿＿＿＿＿＿＿＿＿＿＿＿

＿＿＿＿＿＿＿＿＿＿＿＿＿＿＿＿＿＿＿＿＿＿＿＿＿＿＿＿＿＿＿＿

2. Preview the vocabulary and notes for Lesson 62.

LESSON 62
Review

1. Read all of the notes for Lesson 62.

2. Yomimashoo!
Read each of the following aloud and then write it in *roomaji*. After you have completely finished, check your own work by finding the answers in the textbook, Interactive Activities Part 1, ❷ of this lesson.

	かんじ	ローマじ		かんじ	ローマじ
1	田中さん		13	四年生	
2	書きます		14	十万人	
3	目と耳		15	言いました	
4	中国語と日本語		16	六年前	
5	お父さんのお名前		17	母のお金	
6	雨と雪		18	読みました	
7	元気な子ども		19	聞きます	
8	来年の四月三日		20	八つ	
9	東京駅		21	日本の大学	
10	千百五十一円		22	高校の先生	
11	私の小学校		23	今日の天気	
12	上と下		24	何時何分	

Kakimashoo!
Write each of the following sentences in Japanese (*kana* and *kanji*). Use *kanji* for all underlined parts. After you have completely finished, check your work by finding the same sentences in the workbook, Lessons 36 and 48, Writing Practice, ❹.

1. Kongetsu chuugakkoo-no tomodachi-ga futari Nihon-ni ikimasu.

二

2. Kyoo depaato-de kookoo-no nihongo-no sensei-o mimashita.

語

3. Daigaku-no sensei-wa doko-de nihongo-no benkyoo-o shimashita-ka?

語

4. Kotoshi-no 10-gatsu-ni nan-sai-ni narimasu-ka?

十

5. Sono chiisai hon-wa totemo takakatta desu.

85

Optional Writing Practices

1. 山、川
2. 私、天
3. 元、気
4. 田、来
5. 一、二、三、四
6. 五、六、七、八
7. 九、十、上
8. 下、百
9. 千、万
10. 口、目
11. 耳、名
12. 前、父
13. 母、子
14. 言、話
15. 国、語
16. 読、書
17. 聞、間
18. 時、分
19. 雨、雪
20. 東、京
21. 駅

Study, trace and write.

SAN [ZAN] *; yama (mountain)

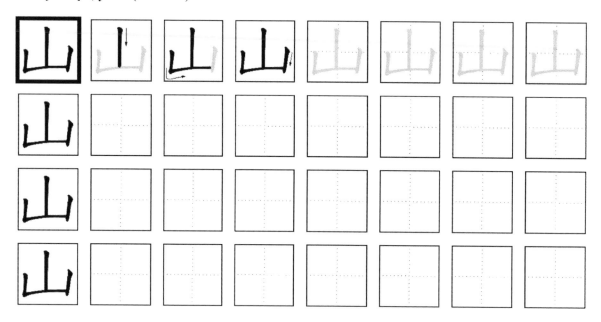

Study, trace and write.

SEN*; kawa [gawa*] (river)

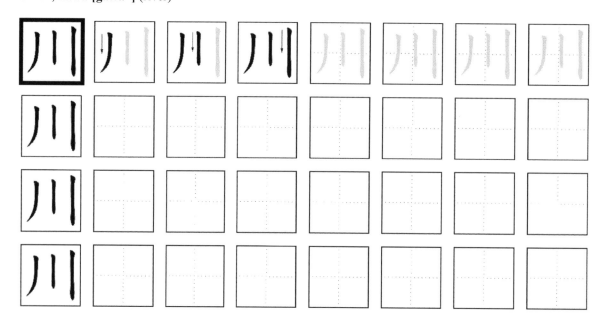

Study, trace and write.

SHI*; watashi, watakushi* (I, privacy)

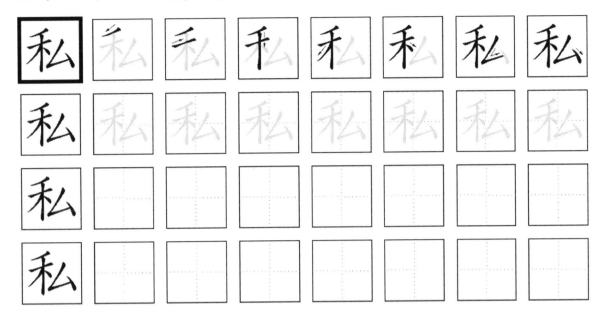

Study, trace and write.

TEN; ame*, ama* (sky, heaven)

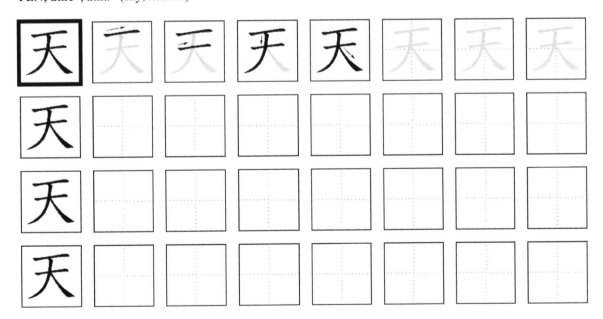

Study, trace and write.

GEN, GAN*; moto* (beginning, foundation)

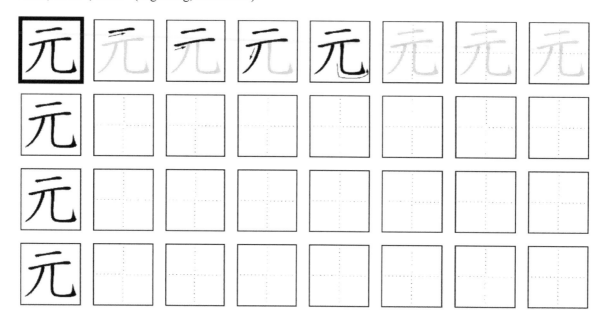

Study, trace and write.

KI, KE* (spirit, energy)

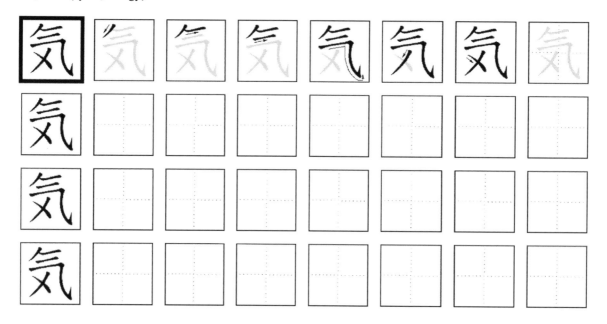

90

Study, trace and write.

DEN*; ta [da] (rice field, paddy)

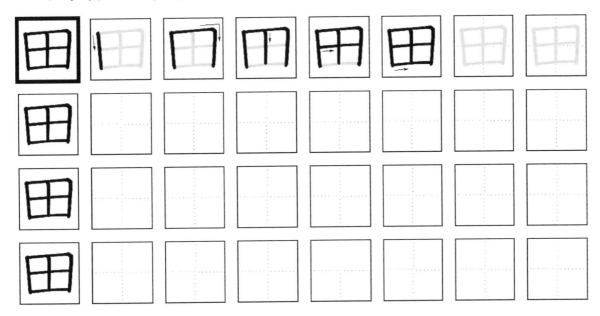

Study, trace and write.

RAI; ku(ru), ki(masu) (come)

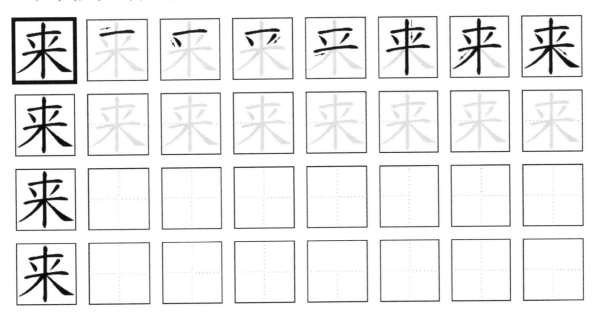

Study, trace and write.

ICHI; hito(tsu) (one)

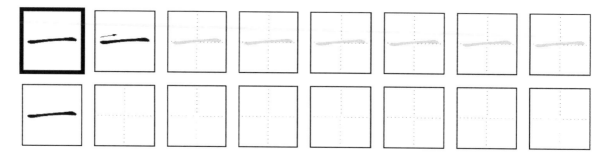

Study, trace and write.

NI; futa(tsu) (two)

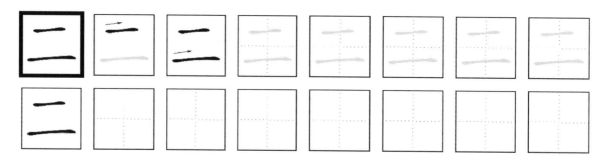

Study, trace and write.

SAN; mit(tsu) (three)

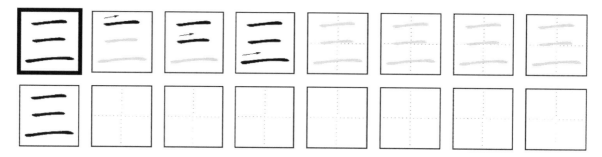

Study, trace and write.

SHI; yon, yo, yot(tsu) (four)

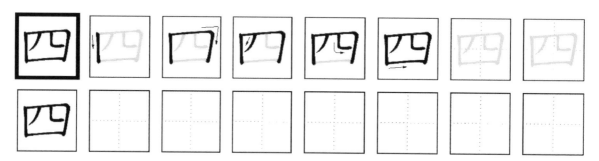

Study, trace and write.

GO; itsu(tsu) (five)

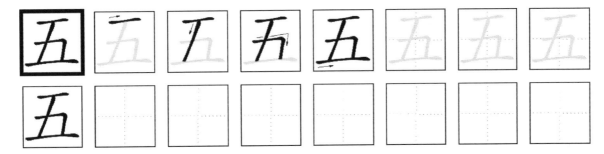

Study, trace and write.

ROKU; mut(tsu) (six)

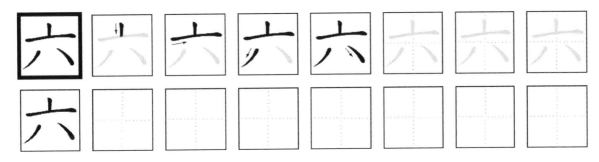

Study, trace and write.

SHICHI; nana(tsu) (seven)

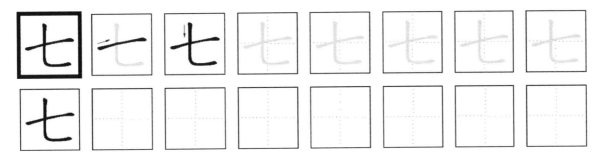

Study, trace and write.

HACHI; yat(tsu) (eight)

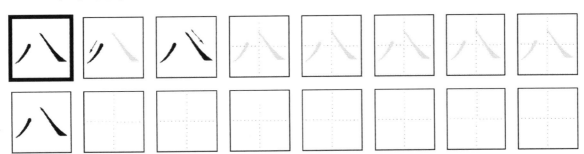

Study, trace and write.

KU, KYUU; kokono(tsu) (nine)

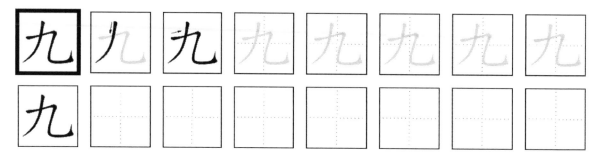

Study, trace and write.

JUU; too (ten)

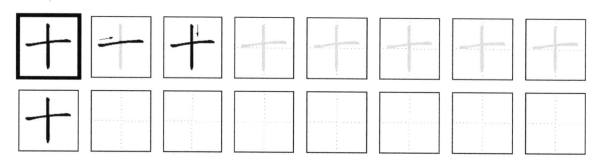

Study, trace and write.

JOO*; ue (top, up, above, over), **kami*** (upper), **a(geru)*** (raise), **a(garu)*** (rise)

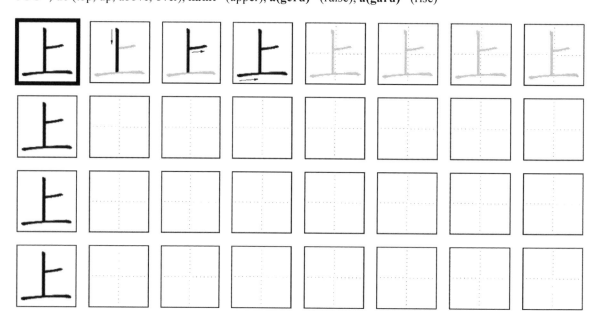

Study, trace and write.

KA*, GE*; shita (bottom, down, under), **shimo*** (lower), **sa(geru)*** (hang, lower), **sa(garu)*** (hang down), **kuda(saru)** (give me)

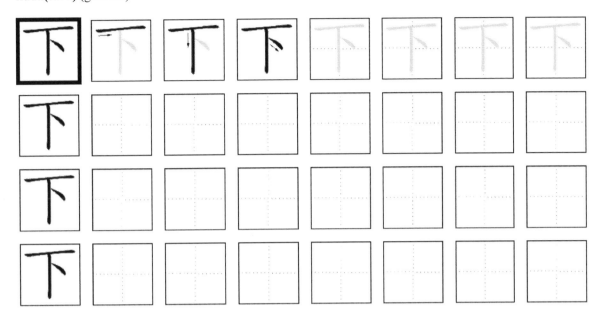

Study, trace and write.

HYAKU [BYAKU, PYAKU] (hundred)

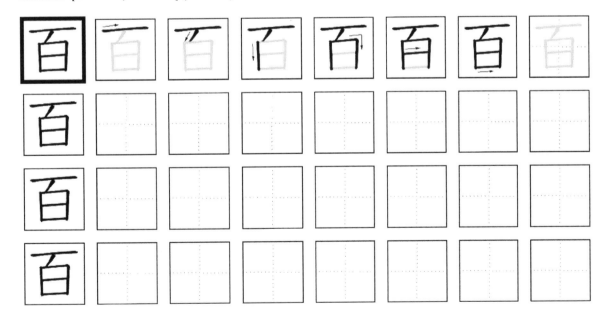

Study, trace and write.

SEN [ZEN], chi* (thousand)

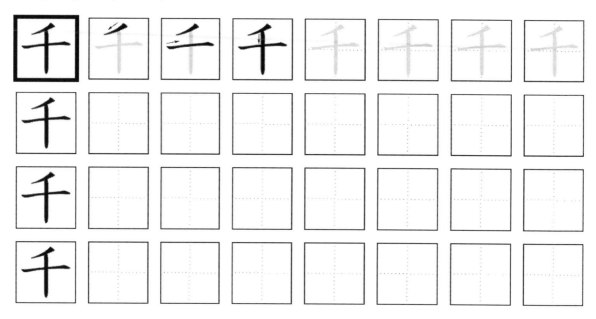

Study, trace and write.

MAN (ten thousand), **BAN***

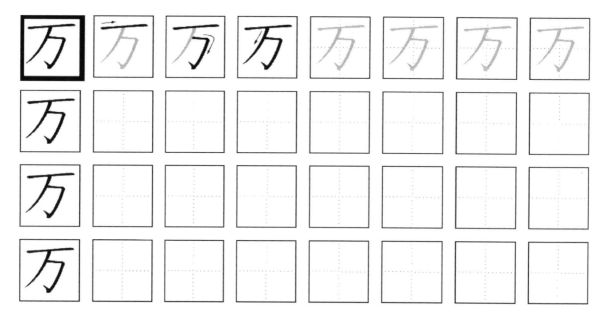

Study, trace and write.

KOO*, KU*; kuchi [guchi] (mouth, opening)

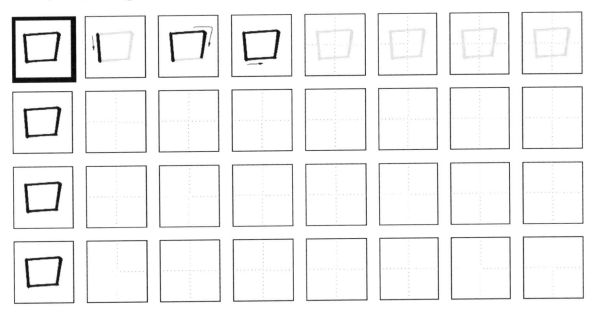

Study, trace and write.

MOKU*; me (eye; *ordinal suffix*)

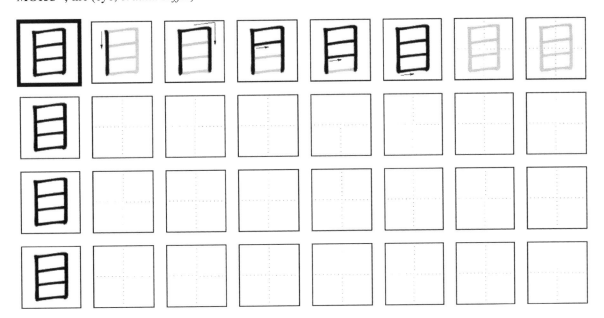

Study, trace and write.

JI*; mimi (ear)

Study, trace and write.

MEI*, MYOO* (name, fame); na (name)

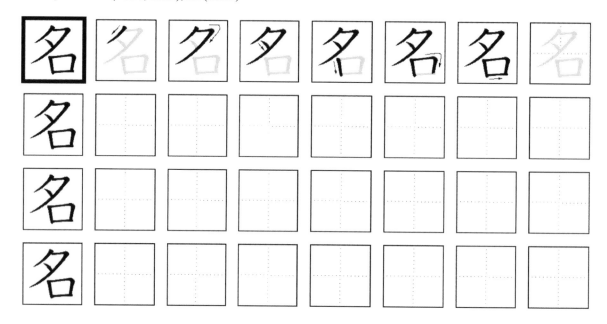

Study, trace and write.

ZEN*; mae (before, front)

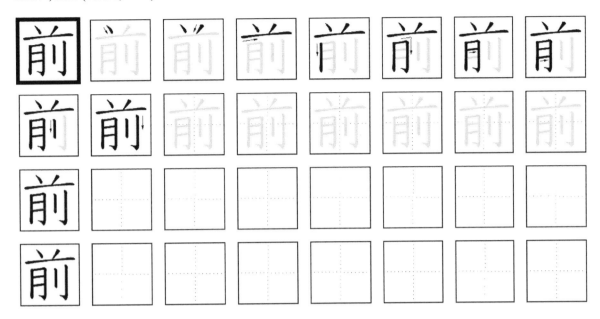

Study, trace and write.

FU*; chichi, (o)too(san) (father)

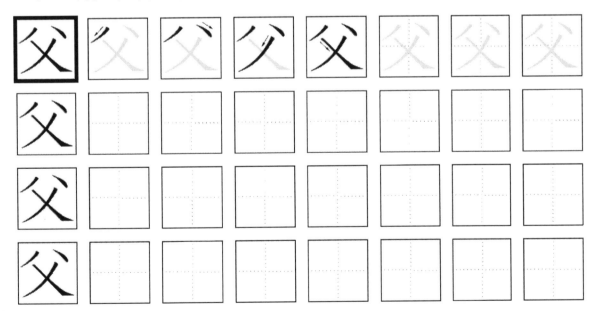

Study, trace and write.

BO*; haha, (o)kaa(san) (mother)

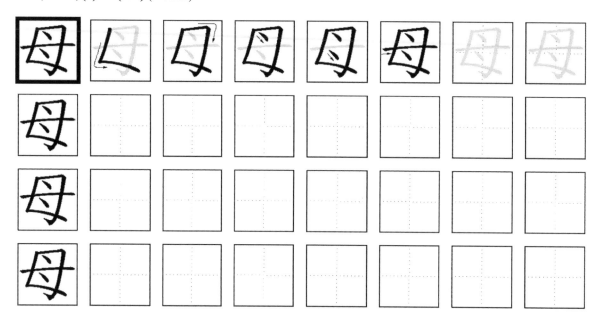

Study, trace and write.

SHI*, SU*; ko [go] (child)

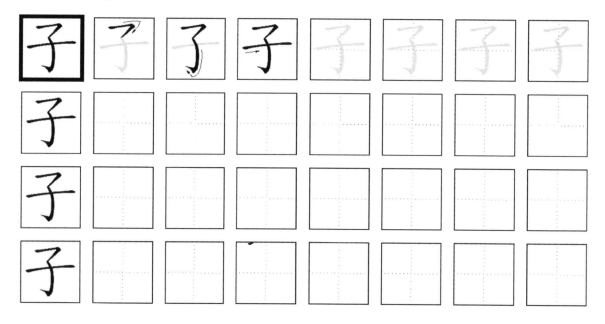

Study, trace and write.

GEN*, **GON*** (speech, statement); **koto*** (word, specch, expression), **i(u)** (say)

Study, trace and write.

WA; hanashi* (story), **hana(su)** (speak)

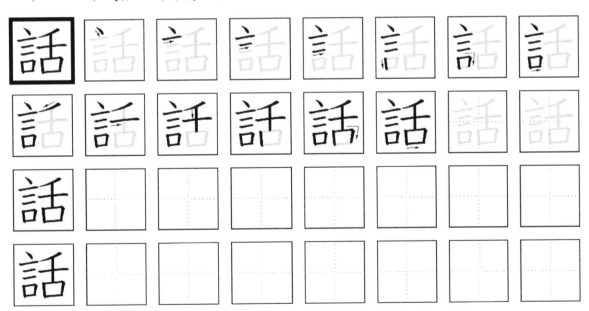

101

Study, trace and write.

KOKU [GOKU]; kuni [guni] (country)

Study, trace and write.

GO (word, speech); **katari [gatari]*** (narration), **kata(ru)*** (tell, speak)

Study, trace and write.

DOKU*, TOKU*; yo(mu) (read)

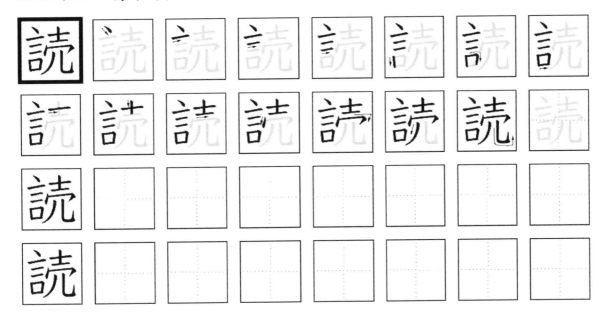

Study, trace and write.

SHO*; ka(ku) (write)

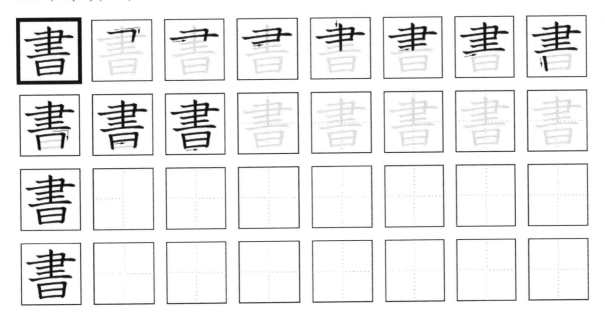

Study, trace and write.

BUN*; ki(ku) (hear, listen to, ask), **ki(koeru)*** (be heard)

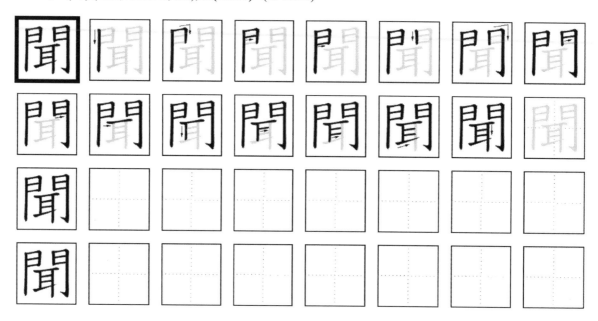

Study, trace and write.

KAN, KEN*; aida* (interval, space), **ma*** (interval, room, time)

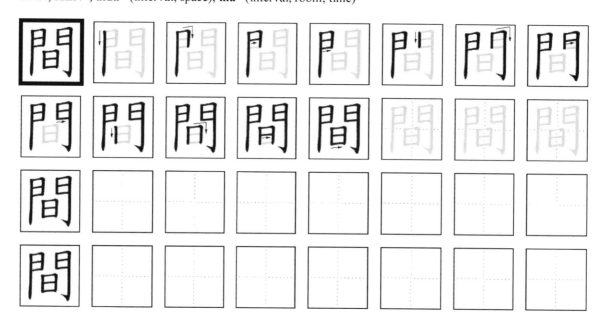

Study, trace and write.

JI; toki [doki] (time, *counter for clock hours*)

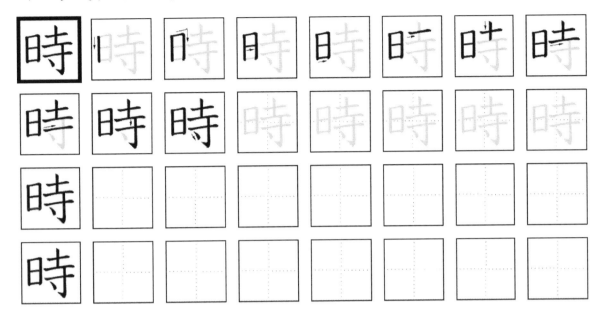

Study, trace and write.

FUN [PUN] (minute, *counter for minutes*), **BUN*, BU*** (part, share); **wa(keru)*** (divide, separate), **wa(karu)** (understand)

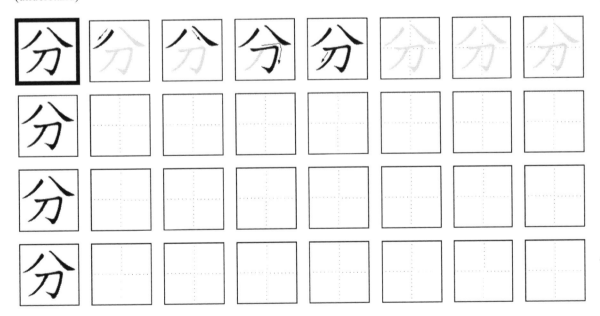

Study, trace and write.

U*; ame, ama* (rain)

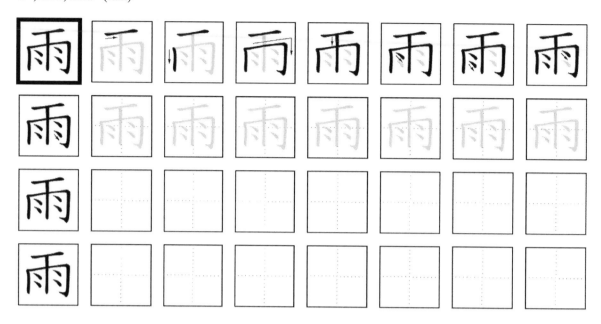

Study, trace and write.

SETSU*; yuki (snow)

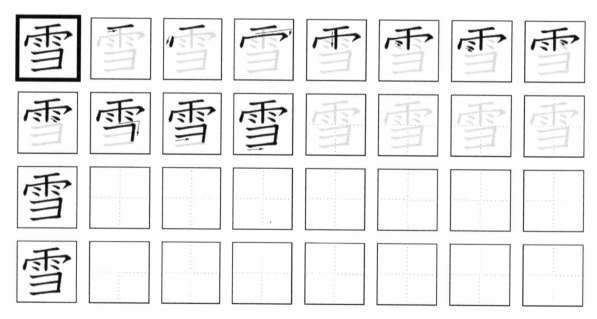

Study, trace and write.

TOO; higashi (east)

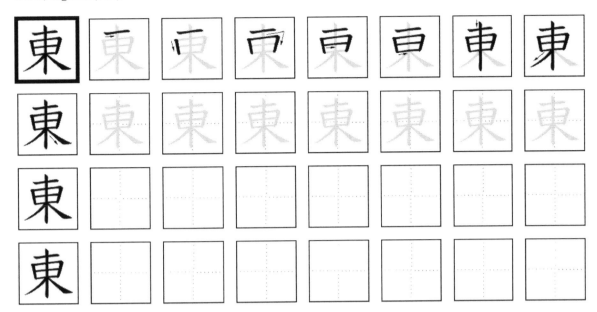

Study, trace and write.

KYOO, KEI* (capital)

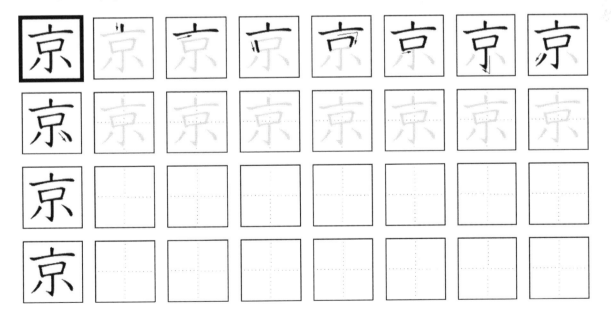

Study, trace and write.

EKI (station)

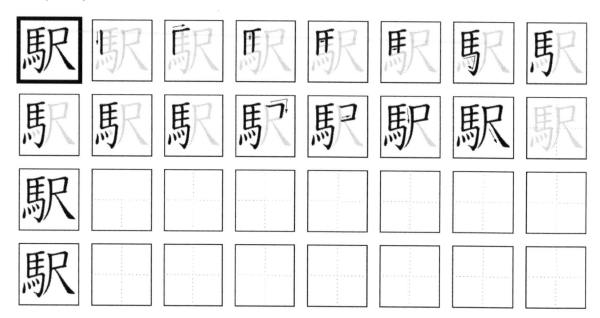

Particle Practices

Particle Practice 1 - (PL. 1- L. 5)

1. Review the following particles and their functions:

   ga: indicating the item which one desires (PL. 1)

   Ex) Kuruma-**ga** hoshii desu. [I want a car.]

   ga: indicating what one is able to do (with *dekimasu*) (PL. 2, L. 1)

   Ex) Tenisu-**ga** dekimasu. [I can play tennis.]

   ga: indicating what is liked/pleasing or disliked/displeasing (PL. 2, L. 1)

   Ex) Nihongo-**ga** suki desu. [I like the Japanese language.]

   kara: indicating the point in time when activities begin (L. 2)

   made: indicating the point in time when activities end (L. 2)

   Ex) Jugyoo-wa 9-ji-**kara** 10-ji-**made** desu. [The class is from 9:00 to 10:00.]

   ni: indicating the time or occasion when an action or process occurs (L. 2)

   Ex) Roku-gatsu-**ni** nihon-ni ikimasu. [I will go to Japan in June.]

   no: indicating possession of the item that follows it by the person who precedes it (L. 4)

   Ex) Yamada-san-**no** baiku desu. [It is Ms. / Mr. Yamada's motorcycle.]

   o: indicating the direct object of a sentence (with *katte-imasu*) (L. 4)

   Ex) Watashi-wa neko-**o** katte-imasu. [I have a cat.]

2. Choose the appropriate particle from the box and fill in the blanks.

   a) Sukii-(   ) dekimasu-ka? [Can you ski?]

   b) Eiga-wa 8-ji 5-fun-(   ) 9-ji 50-pun-(   ) desu. [The movie is from 8:05 to 9:50.]

   c) Fuyu-yasumi-(   ) Hawai-ni ikimasu. [I will go to Hawaii in the winter break.]

   d) O-tanjoobi-(   ) nani-(   ) hoshii desu-ka? [What do you want for your birthday?]

   e) Ichiroo-kun-(   ) jisho desu-ka? [Is it Ichiro's dictionary?]

   f) Haru-(   ) suki desu. [I like spring.]

   g) Boku-wa inu-(   ) katte-imashita. [I had a dog.]

made	ni	kara	ga	no	o

3. Complete the following dialogues by filling in the blanks with an appropriate particle.

   a) A: Supootsu-(   ) nani-(   ) suki-desu-ka?

      B: Gorufu-(   ) suki desu.

      A: Watashi-mo gorufu-(   ) suki desu-yo.

      B: Jaa, haru-yasumi-(   ) gorufu-(   ) shimasen-ka?

      A: Ii desu-ne.

   b) A: Kenji-kun, petto-(   ) katte-imasu-ka?

      B: Iie, katte-imasen.

      A: Petto-(   ) hoshii desu-ka?

      B: Hai, inu-(   ) hoshii desu.

110

c) A: Rika-san, 6-gatsu-(   ) 8-gatsu-(   ) Nihon-(   ) ikimashita-ne.

  B: Hai, soo desu.

  A: Nihon-(   ) nani-(   ) shimashita-ka?

  B: Nihonjin-no tomodachi-(   ) Kyuushuu-(   ) ikimashita.

  A: Hee.

Particle Practice 2 - (L. 6-15)

1. Review important particles and their functions:

  o: indicating the direct object of a sentence (L. 6)

     Ex) Eigo-**o** hanashimasu. [I speak English.]

  de: indicating the place where an action occurs (L. 6)

  wa: indicating the topic of a sentence; often used in conjunction with another particle, as **de** above (L. 6)

     Ex) Kanada-**de-wa** eigo-to furansugo-o hanashimasu. Nihon-**de-wa** nihongo-o hanashimasu.

     [They speak English and French in Canada. They speak Japanese in Japan.]

  kara: indicating a given time or place from which something or someone originates (L. 7)

     Ex) Dochira-**kara** desu-ka? [Where are you from?]

  no: indicating the modification of the noun that follows it by the noun that precedes it (L. 7)

     Ex) Nihon-**no** dochira-kara desu-ka? [Where in Japan are you from?]

     Ex) Mekishiko-wa Amerika-**no** minami-ni arimasu. [Mexico is south of the U.S.]

  de: pinpointing a physical space (with *ichiban*) (L. 9)

     Ex) Fuji-san-wa Nihon-**de** ichiban takai yama desu. [Mt. Fuji is the highest mountain in Japan.]

  de: indicating an exclusive agent (with *jibun*) (L. 11)

     Ex) Jibun-**de** suugaku-no-shukudai-o shimasu. [(I) will do my math homework by myself.]

  ni: indicating the place/area where something or someone exists (with *haitte-iru*) (L. 14)

     Ex) Tenisu-bu-**ni** haitte-imasu. [I belong to the tennis club.] (L. 14)

2. Choose the appropriate particle from the box and fill in the blanks.

  a) A: Burajiru-(   )-(   ) nani-go-(   ) hanashimasu-ka?

    [What language do they speak in Brazil?]

    B: Porutogarugo-(   ) hanashimasu. [They speak Portuguese.]

  b) Joojia-(   ) Atoranta-(   ) desu. [I am from Atlanta, GA.]

  c) Kanada-wa Amerika-(   ) kita-(   ) arimasu. [Canada is north of the U.S.]

  d) Amerika-(   ) ichiban nagai kawa-wa Mishishippii-gawa desu.

    [The longest river in the U.S. is the Mississippi River.]

kara	wa	de	no	ni	o

3. Complete the following dialogues by filling in the blanks with an appropriate particle.

    a) A: Yuka-san, kurabu-(　　　　　) haitte imasu-ka?

       B: Iie, haitte-imasen. Mainichi, arubaito-(　　　　　) shimasu. Miki-san-wa?

       A: Watashi-wa basukettobooru-bu-(　　　　　) haitte-imasu.

       B: Kurabu-wa doo desu-(　　　　　)?

       A: Omoshiroi desu-yo.

    b) A: Jon-kun-wa nani-go-(　　　　　) dekimasu-ka?

       B: Nihongo-(　　　　　) supeingo-(　　　　　) dekimasu.

       A: Hee, sugoi desu-ne. Doko-(　　　　　) benkyoo-o shimashita-ka?

       B: Kookoo-(　　　　　) nihongo-no benkyoo-o shimashita. Supeingo-wa jibun-(　　　　　)

          benkyoo-o shimashita.

       A: Hee.

    c) A: Suisu-(　　　　　) doko-ni arimasu-ka?

       B: Furansu-(　　　　　) higashi-(　　　　　) arimasu.

       A: Suisu-(　　　　　)-(　　　　　) nani-go-(　　　　　) hanashimasu-ka?

       B: Doitsugo-(　　　　　) furansugo-(　　　　　) itariago-(　　　　　) hanashimasu.

       A: Jaa, Suisu-(　　　　　) ichiban kireina yama-wa nan desu-ka?

       B: Mattaahorun desu.

Particle Practice 3 - (L. 16-23)

1. Review the following particles and their functions:

   ni: indicating the place/area where something or someone exists (L. 16)

          Ex) Hon-wa tsukue-no ue-**ni** arimasu. [The book is on the desk.]

   ni: indicating the person one meets (with *au*) (L. 18)

          Ex) Nihongo-no-sensei-**ni** aimasu. [I will meet with my Japanese teacher.]

   ni: indicating the indirect object (an addressee) of a sentence whom something is directed towards (L. 20)

          Ex) Tomodachi-**ni** tegami-o kakimashita. [I wrote a letter to my friend.]

   e: indicating the place of going, the direction of movement (L. 21)

          Ex) Ashita Tookyoo-**e** ikimasu. [I will go to Tokyo tomorrow.]

   o: indicating the direct object of a sentence (L. 19)

          Ex) Watashi-wa shuumatsu e-**o** kakimasu. [I paint/draw pictures on weekends.]

   e: indicating the person who is addressed at the beginning of a letter; meaning "To ~" (L. 21)

          Ex) Kazuko-san-**e** [To Kazuko,]

2. Choose the appropriate particle from the box and fill in the blanks.

    a) Tomomi-san-(　　　　) [Dear Tomomi,]

    b) Do-yoobi-ni booifurendo-(　　　　　) aimasu. [I will see my boyfriend on Saturday.]

    c) Haru-yasumi-ni Mekishiko-(　　　　　) ikimasu. [I will go to Mexico over the spring break.]

d) Neko-wa isu-no shita-( ) imasu. [The cat is under the chair.]

e) Shumi-wa kitte-( ) atsumeru-koto desu. [My hobby is collecting stamps.]

ni	e	o

3. Complete the following dialogues by filling in the blanks with an appropriate particle.

a) A: Fuyu-yasumi-wa moo sugu desu-ne. Noriko-san-wa nani-( ) shimasu-ka?

B: Amerika-ni itte, tomodachi-( ) aimasu.

A: Hee, ii desu-ne. Tomodachi-wa doko-( ) imasu-ka?

B: Furorida-( ) imasu.

A: Aa, soo desu-ka.

b) A: Shumi-wa nan desu-ka?

B: Ryokoo-( ) suru-koto-( ) shashin-( ) toru-koto desu.

A: Natsu-( ) doko-( ) ikimashita-( )?

B: Chuugoku-( ) Nihon-( ) ikimashita.

c) A: Senshuu-no nichi-yoobi-( ) nani-( ) shimashita-ka?

B: Nihonjin-no tomodachi-( ) kaado [card]-( ) kakimashita.

A: Sorekara, nani-ka shimashita-ka?

B: Ee, ane-no uchi-( ) ikimashita.

A: Oneesan-no uchi-wa doko-( ) arimasu-ka?

B: Atoranta-( ) minami-( ) arimasu.

Particle Practice 4 - (L. 24-31)

1. Review the following particles and their functions:

de: indicating boundaries of time (with *ato*) (L. 24)

Ex) Mata, ato-**de** kimasu. [I will come back here again later.]

no: indicating a description or modification of the noun that follows it by the noun that precedes it (L. 25, L. 27)

ni: indicating the time or occasion when an action or process occurs (L. 25)

Ex) Raishuu, tenisu-**no** shiai-ga arimasu. [I will have a tennis match next week.]

Ex) Rainen-**no** 8-gatsu-**ni** ryokoo-o shimasu. [I will travel (somewhere) next August.]

ga: indicating the subject of a sentence; used with question words and their answers (L. 27)

Ex) Q: Dare-**ga** kachimashita-ka?　A: Yamada-san-**ga** kachimashita.

[Q: Who won?　A: Mr. Yamada won.]

ni: indicating the place or purpose of going, the direction of movement (L. 28, L. 29)

Ex) Doko-**ni** asobi-**ni** ikitai desu-ka? [Where do you want to go (to have fun)?]

wa: indicating the topic of the sentence (L. 31)

ni: indicating where something or someone exists (L. 31)

Ex) Depaato-**wa** doko-**ni** arimasu-ka? [Where is the department store?]

2. Choose the appropriate particle from the box and fill in the blanks.

  a) Ashita, uchi-(   ) asobi-(   ) kimasen-ka?

      [Would you like to come to my place (to have fun) tomorrow?]

  b) Sakana-ya-(   ) doko-(   ) arimasu-ka? [Where is the fish store?]

  c) Ato-(   ) sakkaa-(   ) renshuu-o shimasu. [I will practice soccer laer.]

  d) Kyonen-(   ) fuyu sukii-(   ) ikimashita. [I went skiing last winter.]

  e) Konshuu, basukettobooru-(   ) shiai-(   ) arimasu-ka?

      [Are there any basketball games this week?]

wa	no	ga	ni	de

3. Complete the following dialogues by filling in the blanks with an appropriate particle.

  a) (Person A is asking Person B for directions using a map.)

      A: Kono machi-(   ) niku-ya-(   ) arimasu-ka?

      B: Hai, arimasu.

      A: Doko-(   ) arimasu-ka?

      B: Kooen-(   ) hidari-(   ) arimasu.

      A: Doomo.

  b) A: Moshi moshi? Irasshai Kookoo-(   ) Timu desu kedo, Miki-san-(   )

          irasshaimasu-(   )?

      B: Aa, sumimasen. Ima rusu desu kedo.

      A: Aa, soo desu-ka. Nan-ji-goro okaeri desu-(   )?

      B: Hachi-ji goro kaerimasu.

      A: Jaa, mata ato-(   ) denwa shimasu.

      B: Hai, wakarimashita.

      A: Shitsurei shimasu.

  c) A: Makoto-kun, kongetsu-(   ) 11-nichi, hima desu-ka?

      B: Hai, hima desu.

      A: Watashi-(   ) uchi-(   ) paatii-(   ) shimasu kedo,

          asobi-(   ) kimasen-(   )?

      B: Aa, ii desu-ne.

  d) A: Kinoo-(   ) yakyuu-(   ) shiai-wa doo deshita-(   )?

      B: Yokatta desu-yo.

      A: Doko-(   ) kachimashita-(   )?

      B: Raionzu-(   ) kachimashita.

      A: Sukoa-wa doo deshita-(   )?

      B: 5 tai 3 deshita.

      A: Hee.

Particle Practice 5 - (L. 32-40)

1. Review the following particles and their functions:

ga: indicating the subject of a sentence; used with question words and their answers (with *dotchi, kotchi, sotchi, atchi* + adjective) (L. 32)

Ex) Q: Dotchi-**ga** ii desu-ka?   A: Kotchi-**ga** ii desu.

[Q: Which one do you prefer?   A: I prefer this one.]

ni: indicating the result of deciding or choosing (with *suru*) (L. 32)

Ex) Piza-**ni** shimashoo! [Let's have pizza!]

ni: indicating the place/area where something or someone exists (L. 33)

ga: indicating the subject of a sentence (with *aru* or *iru*) (L. 33)

Ex) Kono chikaku-**ni** hon-ya-**ga** arimasu-ka? [Is there a bookstore nearby?]

kara: indicating a given place from which something is described (L. 33, 34)

no: indicating a description or modification of the noun that follows it by the noun that precedes it (L. 33, L. 34)

Ex) Gakkoo-wa uchi-**kara** tooi desu. [The school is far from my house.]

Ex) Hidari-**kara** 2-ban-me-**no** keeki-o 3-tsu kudasai. [Please give me three of the cakes that are second from the left.]

o: indicating the direct object of a sentence (L. 35)

Ex) Shashin-**o** misete kudasai. [Please show me your picture.]

kara: indicating the source of an action (with *morau*) (L. 35)

Ex) Chichi-**kara** kuruma-**o** moraimashita. [I got a car from my father.]

ni: indicating the time or occasion when an action or process occurs (with *mae*) (L. 35)

Ex) 3-nen mae-**ni** Nihon-ni ikimashita. [I went to Japan three years ago.]

ga: indicating what is needed (with *iru*) (L. 36)

Ex) Supuun-**ga** 4-hon irimasu. [I need four spoons.]

ga: indicating what is experienced (with *aru*) (L. 39)

Ex) Sukii-o shita koto-**ga** arimasu-ka? [Have you ever skied?]

2. Choose the appropriate particle from the box and fill in the blanks.

no		ni
ga		o
kara		

a) Dotchi-(   ) yasui desu-ka? [Which one is cheaper?]

b) Dore-(   ) shimashoo-ka? [Which one should we choose?]

c) Eki-wa koko-(   ) tooi desu-ka? [Is the train station far from here?]

d) Kono chikaku-(   ) yuubinkyoku-(   ) arimasu-ka? [Is there a post office nearby?]

e) Migi-(   ) 3-ban-me-(   ) tokei-(   ) misete kudasai.

[Please show me the third watch from the right.]

f) Ni-nen mae-(   ) ane-(   ) kono hon-(   ) moraimashita.

[I got this book from my sister two years ago.]

g) Nani-(   ) irimasu-ka? [What do you need?]

h) Gaikoku-ni itta koto-(   ) arimasu-ka? [Have you ever been to a foreign country?]

115

3. Complete the following dialogues by filling in the blanks with an appropriate particle.

a) A: Irasshaimase.

   B: Migi-(   ) 3-ban-me-(   ) kamera-(   ) misete kudasai.

   A: Hai, doozo.

   B: Ikura desu-ka?

   A: 25,000-en desu.

b) A: Sumimasen. Kono chikaku-(   ) suupaa-(   ) arimasu-ka?

   B: Iie, arimasen.

   A: Soo desu-ka. Jaa, pan-ya-(   ) arimasu-ka?

   B: Hai, ano toshokan-(   ) tonari-(   ) arimasu.

c) A: Fuyu-yasumi-(   ) nani-(   ) shimashita-ka?

   B: Kazoku-(   ) sukii-(   ) ikimashita. A-san-wa sukii-(   ) shita koto-(   ) arimasu-ka?

   A: Iie, arimasen. Sukii-(   ) doo deshita-ka?

   B: Totemo muzukashikatta desu.

d) A: Kyoo sandoitchi-(   ) tsukurimasu-kedo, nani-(   ) irimasu-ka?

   B: Tomato-(   ) 2-tsu-(   ) pan-(   ) irimasu.

e) A: Irasshaimase.

   [Person B is showing the store clerk, A, a catalogue of stereos.]

   B: Kono sutereo-(   ) arimasu-ka?

   A: Hai, kuro-(   ) ao-(   ) arimasu-kedo, dotchi-(   ) ii desu-ka?

   B: Jaa, kuro, onegai shimasu.

   A: Hai, arigatoo gozaimasu.

f) A: O-tanjoobi-(   ) doo deshita-ka?

   B: Yokatta desu-yo. Ani-(   ) purezento-(   ) moraimashita.

   A: Nani-(   ) moraimashita-ka?

   B: Kono kutsu-(   ) moraimashita.

   A: A, kakkoii desu-ne.

Particle Practice 6 - (L. 41-48)

1. Review the following particles and their functions:

ga: indicating the subject of a sentence (L. 42, L. 44)

   Ex) Atama-**ga** itai-n desu. [My head hurts.]

   Ex) Netsu-**ga** aru-n desu. [I have a fever. (lit. A fever exists.)]

   Ex) Kami-**ga** nagai desu-ne. [Your hair is long, isn't it?]

no: indicating the modification of the noun that follows it by the noun that precedes it (L. 44, L. 47)

ni: indicating the time or occasion when an action or process occurs (with *mae*) (L. 44)

116

de: indicating boundaries of time (with *ato*) (L. 44)

    Ex) Jugyoo-**no** mae-**ni** shukudai-o shimasu. [I do homework before class.]

    Ex) Ofuro-**no** ato-**de** nemasu. [I go to bed after taking a bath.]

    Ex) Ano sukaato-**no** hito-wa dare desu-ka? [Who is that person over there wearing a skirt?]

o: indicating the direct object of a sentence (L. 47)

    Ex) Maki-san-wa megane-**o** shite-imasu. [Maki is wearing glasses.]

2. Choose the appropriate particle from the box and fill in the blanks.

    a) Nodo-(   ) itai-n desu. [My throat hurts.]

    b) Arubaito-(   ) mae-(   ) ban-gohan-o tabemasu. [I eat dinner before going to my part-time job.]

    c) Gohan-(   ) ato-(   ) terebi-o mimashita. [I watched TV after the meal.]

    d) Oniisan-wa se-(   ) takai desu-ka? [Is your brother tall?]

    e) Ano akai nekutai-(   ) hito-wa Suzuki-sensei desu.

    [That person over there with the red tie is Dr. Suzuki.]

    f) Suzuki-sensei-wa megane-(   ) shite-imasu-ka? [Does Dr. Suzuki wear glasses?]

ga	de	no	ni	o

3. Complete the following dialogues by filling in the blanks with an appropriate particle.

    a) A: Doo shita-n desu-ka?

      B: Onaka-(   ) itai-n desu.

      A: Itsu-(   ) desu-ka?

      B: Kyoo-(   ) asa-(   ) desu.

      A: Soo desu-ka. Ja, kore-(   ) nonde kudasai.

      B: Itsu kono kusuri-(   ) nomimasu-ka?

      A: Gohan-(   ) mae-(   ) nonde kudasai.

    b) A: Eigo-(   ) sensei-(   ) o-namae-(   ) nan desu-ka?

      B: Tanaka-sensei desu.

      A: Tanaka-sensei-(   ) donna hito desu-ka?

      B: Se-(   ) takakute kami-(   ) nagai hito desu.

      A: Tanaka-sensei-(   ) megane-(   ) shite-imasu-ka?

      B: Iie, shite-imasen.

      A: Tanaka-sensei-(   ) ano kuroi jaketto-(   ) hito desu-ka?

      B: Hai, soo desu.

Particle Practice 7 - (L. 49-56)

1. Review the following particles and their functions:

ni: indicating the time or occasion when an action or process occurs (L. 49)

    Ex) Senshuu-no nichi-yoobi-**ni** umaremashita. [He was born last Sunday.]

de: indicating the place where an action occurs (L. 49, L. 52)

    Ex) Kanada-**de** umaremashita. [I was born in Canada.]

    Ex) Nihon-no kaisha-**de** hataraite-imasu. [I work in a Japanese company.]

ni: indicating where something or someone exists (with *sunde-iru*) (L. 50)

    Ex) Ima Nihon-**ni** sunde-imasu. [I live in Japan now.]

no: indicating the modification of the noun that follows it by the noun that precedes it (L. 50)

    Ex) Kodomo-**no** toki Igirisu-ni sunde-imashita. [I lived in England when I was child.]

de: indicating an exclusive agent (with *hitori*) (L. 51)

    Ex) Ima hitori-**de** sunde-imasu. [I live alone now.]

ni: indicating the time or occasion when an action takes place (with *go*) (L. 54)

    Ex) Ni-nen-go-**ni** kekkon shimasu. [I will get married in two years.]

o: indicating a place from which someone leaves (with *sotsugyoo suru*) (L. 54)

    Ex) Kotoshi chuugakkoo-**o** sotsugyoo shimasu. [I will graduate from middle school this year.]

ni: indicating the result of a course of events, a change (with *naru*) (L. 55)

    Ex) Shoorai isha-**ni** narimasu. [I will become a doctor in the future.]

2. Choose the appropriate particle from the box and fill in the blanks.

  a) Yamashita-san-no akachan-wa asa-no 3-ji-(   ) Minami Byooin-(   ) umaremashita.

    [Mrs. Yamashita's baby was born at 3:00 in the morning at Minami Hospital.]

  b) Shoogaku-sei-(   ) toki, Shikago-(   ) sunde-imashita.

    [I lived in Chicago when I was an elementary school student.]

no	ni	de	o

  c) Kookoo-sei-(   ) toki, hitori-(   ) Furansu-ni ikimashita.

    [I went to France by myself when I was a high school student.]

  d) Eri-san-wa 3-nen-go-(   ) daigaku-(   ) sotsugyoo shimasu.

    [Eri will graduate from college in three years.]

  e) Otoosan-wa doko-(   ) hataraite-imasu-ka? [Where does your father work?]

  f) Shoorai bengoshi-(   ) naritai desu. [I want to be a lawyer in the future.]

3. Complete the following dialogues by filling in the blanks with an appropriate particle.

  a) A: Makoto-kun-(   ) doko-(   ) umaremashita-ka?

    B: Tokyo-(   ) umaremashita.

    A: Tokyo-(   ) dore gurai sunde-imashita-ka?

    B: 3-sai-(   ) toki-made sunde-imashita.

  b) A: Kyonen-(   ) natsu yasumi-(   ) nani-(   ) shimashita-ka?

    B: Hawai-(   ) ikimashita.

    A: Dare-(   ) ikimashita-ka?

    B: Hitori-(   ) ikimashita.

    A: Hawai-(   ) nani-(   ) shimashita-ka?

    B: Hoteru-(   ) hatarakimashita.

c) A: Michiko-san-(   ) itsu daigaku-(   ) sotsugyoo shimasu-ka?

   B: 2-nen-go-(   ) sotsugyoo shimasu.

   A: Sorekara, nani-(   ) shimasu-ka?

   B: Gakkoo-(   ) sensei-(   ) naritai desu.

Particle Practice 8 - (L. 57-63)

1. Review the following particles and their functions:

   ni: indicating where something or someone exists (with *iru*) (L. 57)

   Ex) Kamakura-**ni** mikka-kan imashita. [I was in Kamakura for three days.]

   ni: indicating the time or occasion when an action or process occurs (L. 58)

   Ex) 3-ji-**ni** tsukimasu / demasu. [I will arrive / leave at 3:00.]

   ga: indicating what is needed (with *iru*) (L. 58)

   Ex) Ryokoo-ni pasupooto-**ga** irimasu. [I need a passport for my trip.]

   o: indicating the direct object of a sentence (L. 59, L. 61)

   ni: indicating where something or someone exists (with *wasureru*) (L. 59, L. 61)

   Ex) Koko-de shashin-**o** totte-mo ii desu-ka? [May I take a photo here?]

   Ex) Kaban-**o** sagashite-imasu. [I'm looking for my bag.]

   Ex) Resutoran-**ni** hon-**o** wasuremashita. [I left (my) book at the restaurant.]

   ni: indicating the place of arrival or the direction of movement (with *tsuku*) (L. 60)

   Ex) 8-ji-ni gakkoo-**ni** tsukimashita. [I arrived at the school at 8:00.]

   o: indicating the point of departure (with *deru*) (L. 60)

   Ex) Itsu koko-**o** demasu-ka? [When are you leaving here?]

   made: indicating the destination of movement; meaning "until, to, up to" (L. 60)

   Ex) Hakone-**made** 1-mai kudasai. [Please give me one ticket for Hakone.]

   ga: indicating the subject of a sentence (with *nakunaru*) (L. 61)

   Ex) Kaban-**ga** nakunarimashita. [My bag has disappeared.]

   ga: indicating the subject of sentence (with *haitte-iru*) (L. 61)

   Ex) Soko-ni nani-**ga** haitte-imasu-ka? [What is in there?]

2. Choose the appropriate particle from the box and fill in the blanks.

   a) Maiami-(   ) 2-shuukan imashita. [I was in Miami for two weeks.]

   b) Gozen 6-ji-(   ) Pari-(   ) tsukimashita. [I arrived in Paris at 6:00 a.m.]

   c) Nan-yoobi-(   ) Tookyoo-(   ) demasu-ka? [On what day are you leaving from Tokyo?]

   d) Kyoo-no paatii-ni keeki-(   ) irimasu. [We need a cake for today's party.]

   e) Doko-de kono shashin-(   ) torimashita-ka? [Where did you take this photo?]

   f) Oosaka-(   ) 2-mai kudasai. [Please give me two tickets to Osaka.]

   g) Megane-(   ) nakunarimashita. Issho-ni megane-(   ) sagashite kudasai. [My glasses are missing. Please look for them with me.]

h) Fudebako-no naka-(   ) keshigomu-to pen-(   ) 3-bon haitte-imasu.

[There is an eraser and three pens in the pencil case.]

i) Kissaten-(   ) kasa-(   ) wasuremashita. [I left my umbrella at the coffee shop.]

made	ni	ga	o

3. Complete the following dialogues by filling in the blanks with an appropriate particle.

a) A: Sengetsu, Furansu-(   ) ikimashita.

B: Hee, ii desu-ne. Itsu Amerika-(   ) demashita-ka?

A: 23-nichi-(   ) gogo 8-ji-(   ) demashita.

B: Soo desu-ka? Itsu Furansu-(   ) tsukimashita-ka?

A: 24-ka-(   ) gozen 10-ji-(   ) tsukimashita.

B: Furansu-(   ) dore gurai imashita-ka?

A: 6-ka-kan imashita.

b) A: Sensei, nihongo-(   ) kyookasho-(   ) nakunarimashita.

B: Soo desu-ka? Kyookasho-wa doko-(   ) arimashita-ka?

A: Kaban-(   ) naka-(   ) haitte-imashita.

B: Sono kaban-wa doko-(   ) arimasu-ka?

A: A, wakarimashita. Tomodachi-no uchi-(   ) sono kaban-(   ) wasuremashita.

irasshai ™
Welcome
to Japanese

Reading and Writing Practices

A. Match the following activities with their corresponding pictures.

1. テニス (   )   2. サッカー (   )   3. ゴルフ (   )   4. バレーボール (   )

a.    b.    c.    d.

B. Write the following activities in *katakana*.

1. _____
    ho o mu su te i (homestay)

3. _____
    do ra i bu (driving)

2. _____
    pi ku ni k ku (picnic)

4. _____
    pa a ti i (party)

C. Fill in the blanks using the given cues. Write in *hiragana*. Write the corresponding *katakana* above the *roomaji*.

1. pool party

_____ に _____ を します。
(birthday)   pu u ru pa a ti i

2.

_____ 、 _____ で _____ を
(weekend)   (home)   te re bi

みました。 _____ の _____ を みました。
      te ni su   ge e mu

3.

_____ に _____ を しました。
(winter break)   su no o bo o do

_____ は とても _____ です。
su no o bo o do

is difficult

D. Read the following passage and answer the questions in English.

　　ぼくは なつやすみに にほんで ホームステイを しました。6月 15日から

8月 14日まで にほんに いました。しゅうまつ、 ホストファミリーの

おにいさんと いっしょに ドライブを しました。ホストファミリーと やまで
　　　　　　　　　　　　　　　　　　　　　　　　　　　　　　　　mountains
ピクニックを しました。とても たのしい なつやすみ でした。

1. What did the writer do during the summer vacation?　　_____

2. From what date until what date did he stay there?

　　He stayed from _____ until _____.

3. What did he do on weekends?　　_____

4. What did he do in the mountains?　　_____

5. What did he think about his experiences there?　　_____

E. Write a similar passage about yourself.

Boku/Watashi-wa _____-ni _____-to _____-ni
　　　　　　　　　　(time word)　　　　(person)　　　　　(the place you went)

ikimashita. _____-kara _____-made ikimashita.
　　　　　　(time word/date)　　　　　　　　　　(time word/date)

_____.
　　　　　　　　　　　　(activity you did there)

_____. Totemo ii ryokoo deshita.
　　(another activity you did there)

F. Now write it in *hiragana*. Write in *katakana* where appropriate.

_____

_____

_____

_____

_____

_____

A. このくには どこですか。Do you know what countries these are? Write the English name of the country next to its *katakana* representation. Then match the famous item with each country from the pictures below.

1. ドイツ _____ ( )   4. イギリス _____ ( )

2. フランス _____ ( )   5. イタリア _____ ( )

3. オーストラリア _____ ( )

a.   b.   c.   d.   e.

B. Crossword Puzzle: Complete the puzzle in *katakana* based on the following clues.

Across
1. Italy (Itaria)
2. Poland (Poorando)
3. Sicily (Shichiria)
4. Australia (Oosutoraria)
5. Kenya (Kenia)

Down
a. Laos (Raosu)
b. Vietnam (Betonamu)
c. Lithuania (Ritoania)
d. Indonesia (Indoneshia)
e. Greece (Girisha)

C. Read the following passage and answer the questions in English.

このくには <u>しま</u> です。ベトナムの ひがしに あります。<u>そして</u>、インドネシア
　　　　　　　　island　　　　　　　　　　　　　　　　　　　　and
の きたに あります。この くには バナナと マンゴと ココナツで <u>ゆうめい</u> です。
　　　　　　　　　　　　　　　　　　　　　　　　　　　　　　　　　famous
この くにの 人は えいごと タガログごを はなします。この くには どこ ですか。

1. Describe the location of this country in relation to two other countries.

It's _____ of _____ and _____ of _____.

2. What is this country famous for?

_____, _____, and _____

3. What languages are spoken here? _____ and _____

4. Based on the information provided in the passage, what country is described here?

_____

D. Write a similar passage about a different country.

Kono kuni-wa _____ desu. _____-no _____-ni
　　　　　　　　　(descriptor)　　　　　(another country)　　(cardinal direction)

arimasu. Soshite, _____-no _____-ni arimasu. Kono kuni-wa
　　　　　　　　　(another country)　　(cardinal direction)

_____-to _____-de yuumei desu. Kono kuni-no
　(famous product)　　　　(famous product)

hito-wa _____-o hanashimasu. Kono kuni-wa doko desu-ka?
　　　　　　(language)

E. Now write it in *hiragana*. Write in *katakana* where appropriate.

_____

_____

_____

_____

_____

_____

A. Fill in the chart by writing appropriate answers in *roomaji* and English in the parentheses.

	Kanji	Reading	Meaning
1.	月	GETSU, ( )	( ), moon
2.	日	( ); -bi, -ka	day, sun, counter for days of the month
3.	木	( ); ki	( ), wood
4.	本	( ), BON, PON	( ), origin, source
5.	人	NIN, JIN; ( ), -ri	person, counter for ( )
6.	山	SAN; ( )	( )
7.	川	( )	( )
8.	大	DAI; ( )-kii	( ), large, great
9.	小	( ); chii-sai	( ), little

B. Choose the appropriate *kanji* from the chart above for the following words and copy the *kanji*.

1. Japan: _____ _____

3. August 7th: 8 _____ 7_____

5. read books: _____をよむ

2. 5 people: 5 _____

4. Thursday: _____よう_____

C. For the questions, fill in the blanks using the cues on the left. Then complete the answers. Write in *hiragana* and *kanji*. Write the corresponding *katakana* above the *roomaji*.

1. in Japan

Q. _____で いちばん たかい 山は なん ですか。
　　　　　　　　　　　さん
A. _____山 です。

2. in North America

Q. _____ _____で いちばん ながい 川は なん ですか。
　　　　A me ri ka　　　　　　　　　がわ
A. _____川です。
　Mi　shi　shi　p　pi　i

3. in the world

Q. _____で いちばん 大きい くには どこ ですか。

A. _____ です。
　Ro　shi　a

D. Read the following passage and answer the questions in English.

わたしの まちは アラスカしゅうに あります。アラスカは カナダの にしに
　　　　　　　　　　　state
あります。アラスカのしゅうとは ジュノーです。アラスカに マッキンリー山が
　　　　　　　　state capital
あります。アラスカで いちばん ながい川は ユーコン川です。アラスカには

みずうみが たくさん あります。

1. Which state is this author's town in?   _____

2. Where is the state located in relationship to Canada? _____ of Canada

3. What is the capital of this state?   _____

4. Write the name of the mountain mentioned here. _____

5. What did the author say about the Yukon River? _____

6. What did the author say about the lakes?   _____

E. Write a similar passage about your own town.

Watashi/Boku-no machi-wa _____-shuu-ni arimasu.
                                    (name of your state)

_____-wa _____-no _____-ni arimasu.
   (your state)   (neighboring state)   (cardinal direction)

_____-no shuuto-wa _____ desu.
   (your state)   (capital of your state)

_____-ni _____-ga arimasu.
   (your state)   (a landmark)

_____-de ichiban _____ _____-wa
   (your state)   (high/long/big, etc.) (a natural feature)

_____ desu.
   (feature's name)

F. Now write it in *hiragana*. Write in *katakana* where appropriate.

_____

_____

_____

_____

_____

_____

A. Fill in the chart by writing appropriate answers in *roomaji* and English in the parentheses.

	Kanji	Reading	Meaning
1.	月	(　　　　　), GATSU	month, (　　　　　)
2.	日	NICHI; -bi, (-　　　)	day, sun, counter for days of the month
3.	小	SHOO; (　　　)-sai	(　　　　　), little
4.	大	(　　　); (　　　)-kii	big, large, great
5.	人	NIN, (　　　　　); hito, -ri	(　　　　　), counter for people
6.	学	(　　　　　)	learning, science
7.	校	KOO	(　　　　　)
8.	中	CHUU; (　　　　)	(　　　　　), inside, within
9.	高	KOO; (　　　)-i	high, (　　　　　)

B. Choose the appropriate *kanji* from the chart above for the following words and copy the *kanji*.

1. one person: 1 _____

2. jr. high school student: _____ 学 せい

3. elementary school: _____ 学校

4. May 5th: 5 _____ 5 _____

5. everyday: まい _____

6. like it very much: _____ すき

C. Fill in the blanks with the appropriate *kanji*. Write the appropriate readings for the underlined *kanji* in the parentheses.

1. _____ よう _____ に 学校 で やきゅう を しました。
　　nichi　　　　bi　　　(　　　　　)

2. _____ ごの じゅぎょうは 2 じかんめ です。
　　ni　　hon

3. 高校 に ともだちが 30 _____ います。
　(　　　　)　　　　　　nin

D. Read the following excerpt from a letter and answer the questions in English. Mika, who lived in the U.S, has returned to Japan. She wrote a letter to Miriam who is studying Japanese.

6 月 20 日

ミリアムさんへ、

　おげんき ですか。なつやすみは どう ですか。
わたしは、いま、テニスぶに はいって います。まい日、クラブが あります。
クラブの メンバーが 16人 います。木よう日の よる、じゅくが あります。
そこで えいごと れきしと すう学の べんきょうを します。まい日 とても
いそがしい です。でも、日本の 高校 が 大すき です。なつやすみは 7月20日に
はじまります。なつやすみが たのしみ です。
　　　　　　　　　　looking forward to

128

1. What is this passage mainly about? Check one of the following.
　　(　) Japanese friends　　(　) Japanese high schools　　(　) Japanese junior high schools

2. What kind of club does Mika belong to?　_____

3. How many members are there in her club?　_____

4. On which day(s) of the week does she attend *juku*?　_____

5. Write three subjects that she studies at *juku*.　_____

6. How does she feel about her school?　_____

7. When does her summer vacation begin?　_____

E. Write a similar passage about yourself.

_____-kara _____-made gakkoo-ni ikimasu.
　　　　(day of the week)　　　　　　　　　　　(day of the week)

_____-no jugyoo-wa _____-jikan-me desu.
　　　　(name of the subject)　　　　　　　　　　(period)

_____-wa _____ desu.
　　　　(name of the subject)　　　　　　　　(adjective to describe the subject)

_____-ni gakkoo-de _____-o shimasu.
　　(days of the week)　　　　　　　　　(name of the activity)

[If you belong to a club] Ima, _____-bu-ni haitte-imasu.
　　　　　　　　　　　　　　　(name of the club)

Watashi/Boku-no gakkoo-ga/wa _____ desu.
　　　　　　　　　　　　　　　(adjective to describe your school)

F. Now write it in *hiragana* and *kanji*. Write in *katakana* where appropriate.

_____

_____

_____

_____

_____

A. Fill in the chart by writing appropriate answers in *roomaji* and English in the parentheses.

	Kanji	Reading	Meaning
1.	何	nan, ( )	( )
2.	大	( ); ( )-kii	( ), large, ( )
3.	校	( )	school
4.	本	HON, ( ), ( )	book, ( ), source
5.	高	( ); taka-i	( ), high
6.	中	( ); naka	middle, ( ), within
7.	学	GAKU	( ), science
8.	人	( ), JIN; hito	( ), counter for people

B. Write the appropriate *kanji* for the following words.

1. How many people?: _____ _____   4. small person: _____ さい_____

2. college: _____ _____   5. Japanese people: _____ _____ _____

3. big book: _____ きい_____

C. Fill in the blanks using the cues from the pictures. Write in *hiragana* and *kanji*. Write the corresponding *katakana* above the *roomaji*.

1.

Q: いま、何を していますか。

A: へやで _____を _____。

2.

Q: だれが いますか。

A: せんせいが 3 _____ _____。

3.

Q: 本だなの うえに 何が ありますか。

A: _____ が _____。
      su   te   re   o

D. Read the following passage and answer the questions in English.

　　わたしの へやに つくえと いすと 本だなと ベッドが あります。つくえの うえに
コンピューターが あります。コンピューターは 高かった です。つくえの ひだりに
大きい 本だなが あります。本だなの 中に まんがと フランスごの 本が たくさん
あります。CDプレーヤーと とけいも あります。いま ベッドの したに 小さい
いぬが います。わたしの へやは きたない です。でも、大すき です。

1. What four pieces of furniture are in this room?

_____, _____, _____, _____

2. Where are two of these pieces of furniture in relation to each other?

_____

3. Where are the French books and the clock? _____

4. Where is the dog? _____

5. Describe the dog. _____

6. How does the author describe her room? _____ but _____

E. Write a similar passage about your own room.

Watashi/Boku-no heya-ni _____ -to _____ -to _____ -ga
　　　　　　　　　　　　　　(furniture)　　　　　　　　(furniture)　　　　　　　(furniture)

arimasu. _____ -wa _____ -no migi/hidari/ue/shita-ni arimasu.
　　　　　　(furniture)　　　　　　　　(furniture)

Heya-de yoku _____.
　　　　　　　　　　　　(what you often do in your room)

Watashi/Boku-no heya-wa/ga _____.
　　　　　　　　　　　　　　　(description: clean, messy, you like it, you don't like it)

F. Now write it in *hiragana* and *kanji*. Write in *katakana* where appropriate.

_____

_____

_____

_____

_____

A. Fill in the chart by writing appropriate answers in *roomaji* and English in the parentheses.

	Kanji	Reading	Meaning
1.	今	KON, (　　　　)	(　　　　), the present
2.	私	(　　　　)	(　　　　), privacy
3.	何	(　　　), nani	(　　　　), how many, *prefix to form questions*
4.	火	(　　　)	(　　　)
5.	水	SUI; (　　　)	(　　　)
6.	金	(　　　); kane	gold, (　　　　)
7.	土	(　　　)	(　　　　), soil

B. Write the appropriate *kanji* for the following words.

1. now: _____　　　　2. today: _____ _____　　　　3. what month?: _____ _____

C. Re-arrange the following days of the week from Sunday through Saturday. Start by putting the number 1 in the parenthesis under "Sunday."

水　　金　　月　　日　　木　　土　　火
(　)　(　)　(　)　(　)　(　)　(　)　(　)

D. Write answers by filling in the blanks using the cues on the left. Write in *hiragana*.

Q. しゅみは 何ですか。

1.

A. _____ を _____ ことです。

2. collecting:

A. _____ を _____ ことです。

3.

A. _____ を _____ ことです。

E. Read the following passage and answer the questions in English.

私の しゅみは りょうりを すること です。しゅうまつ、よく りょうりを

します。このあいだ、ははと アップル・パイを つくりました。土よう日に
　　　　The other day
ストロベリー・ショート・ケーキを つくります。りょうりを することは

むずかしい ですけど、たのしい です。

1. What is the author's hobby?　　　　_____

2. When does she often do this?　　　_____

3. What did she make the other day?　_____

4. Who made it with her?　　　　　　_____

5. What will she make on Saturday?　_____

6. What did she say about her hobby?　_____

F. Write a similar passage about yourself.

Watashi/Boku-no shumi-wa _____ desu.
　　　　　　　　　　　　　　　　(your hobby)

_____ _____.
　　(time word)　　　　　　(activity related to the hobby)

Kono aida, _____-to _____.
　　　　　　　(a person)　　　　(specific thing regarding the hobby)

_____-wa _____.
　　(your hobby)　　　　　　(an adjective to describe the hobby)

G. Now write it in *hiragana* and *kanji*. Write in *katakana* where appropriate.

_____

_____

_____

_____

_____

A. Fill in the chart by writing appropriate answers in *roomaji* and English in the parentheses.

	Kanji	Reading	Meaning
1.	天	( )	( ), heaven
2.	元	( ); moto	beginning, ( )
3.	気	( ), KE	( ), energy
4.	火	( ); hi [bi]	( )
5.	水	( ); mizu	( )
6.	木	( ); ki [gi]	( ), wood

B. Write the appropriate *kanji* for 1 through 3, and write the reading in *hiragana* for 4 and 5.

　1. water: ＿＿＿＿＿　　　3. Thursday: ＿＿よう＿＿　　5. 元気: ＿＿ ＿＿ ＿＿

　2. Tuesday: ＿＿よう＿＿　4. 天気: ＿＿ ＿＿ ＿＿

C. Fill in the blanks using the cues on the left. Write the appropriate season in *hiragana* and the activities in *katakana*.

1. in summer

＿＿＿＿＿＿に ＿＿＿＿＿＿＿＿＿＿を
　　　　　　　　　ba　a　be　kyu　u
します。

2. in winter

＿＿＿＿＿＿に ＿＿＿＿＿＿＿＿＿＿＿
　　　　　　　　ku　ro　su　ka　n　to　ri　i
＿＿＿＿＿＿をします。
su　ki　i

3. in fall

＿＿＿＿＿＿に ＿＿＿＿＿＿＿＿＿＿を
　　　　　　　　pa　n　pu　ki　n　pa　i
たべます。

4. in spring

＿＿＿＿＿＿に ＿＿＿＿＿＿＿＿＿に
　　　　　　　　　pi　ku　ni　k　ku
いきます。

D. Read the following *shochuu-mimai* card and answer the questions in English.

8月 10日 （火よう日）

みきさんへ、
　お元気ですか。サバンナは 今 なつ です。まいにち、とても あつい です けど、
なつが 大すき です。せんしゅうの しゅうまつの 天気は はれ でした。ともだち
と うみに いって、ビーチで バレーボールを しました。たのしかった ですよ。
　みきさんの いちばん すきな きせつは 何ですか。
　みきさん、また てがみを かいてください。さようなら。

エリカ

1. On what day did Erica write this card?　＿＿＿＿＿＿＿＿＿＿＿＿＿＿＿＿＿＿

2. What season is it in Savannah?　＿＿＿＿＿＿＿＿＿＿＿＿＿＿＿＿＿＿

3. How is the weather in Savannah now?　＿＿＿＿＿＿＿＿＿＿＿＿＿＿＿＿＿＿

4. How was the weather last weekend?　＿＿＿＿＿＿＿＿＿＿＿＿＿＿＿＿＿＿

5. What did Erica do last weekend?　＿＿＿＿＿＿＿＿＿＿＿＿＿＿＿＿＿＿

6. What did she say about the activity?　＿＿＿＿＿＿＿＿＿＿＿＿＿＿＿＿＿＿

E. Write a similar card.

＿＿＿＿＿＿-gatsu ＿＿＿＿＿ (＿＿＿＿-yoobi)
　　　　　　　　　　　　　(month)　　　(day)　　(day of the week)

＿＿＿＿＿＿＿＿＿-e,
(name of your pen pal)

O-genki desu-ka? ＿＿＿＿＿＿＿＿＿＿＿＿-wa ima ＿＿＿＿＿＿＿＿＿＿ desu.
　　　　　　　　　(name of your town)　　　　　　　　(current season)

＿＿＿＿＿＿＿＿＿＿＿ desu. Senshuu-no shuumatsu-no tenki-wa ＿＿＿＿＿＿ deshita.
(adjective to describe the weather)　　　　　　　　　　　　(last weekend's weather)

Watashi/Boku-wa ＿＿＿＿＿＿＿＿＿＿＿＿＿＿＿＿＿＿＿＿＿＿＿＿＿.
　　　　　　　　　　(activity you did last weekend)

＿＿＿＿＿＿＿＿＿＿＿＿＿＿. ＿＿＿＿＿＿＿＿＿-no ichiban suki-na
(comment on the activity)　　　(name of your pen pal)

kisetsu-wa nan desu-ka? ＿＿＿＿＿＿＿, mata tegami-o kaite kudasai. Sayoonara.
　　　　　　　　　　(name of your pen pal)

＿＿＿＿＿＿＿＿＿＿
(your name)

F. Now write it in *hiragana* and *kanji*. Write in *katakana* where appropriate.

＿＿＿＿＿＿＿＿＿＿＿＿＿＿＿＿＿＿＿＿＿＿＿＿＿＿＿＿＿＿＿＿＿＿

＿＿＿＿＿＿＿＿＿＿＿＿＿＿＿＿＿＿＿＿＿＿＿＿＿＿＿＿＿＿＿＿＿＿

＿＿＿＿＿＿＿＿＿＿＿＿＿＿＿＿＿＿＿＿＿＿＿＿＿＿＿＿＿＿＿＿＿＿

＿＿＿＿＿＿＿＿＿＿＿＿＿＿＿＿＿＿＿＿＿＿＿＿＿＿＿＿＿＿＿＿＿＿

＿＿＿＿＿＿＿＿＿＿＿＿＿＿＿＿＿＿＿＿＿＿＿＿＿＿＿＿＿＿＿＿＿＿

＿＿＿＿＿＿＿＿＿＿＿＿＿＿＿＿＿＿＿＿＿＿＿＿＿＿＿＿＿＿＿＿＿＿

A. Fill in the chart by writing appropriate answers in *roomaji* and English in the parentheses.

	Kanji	Reading	Meaning
1.	田	DEN; (　　　　) [da]	(　　　　　　　　　)
2.	行	KOO, GYOO; (　　)-ku	(　　　　　　　)
3.	見	KEN; (　　　)-ru	see, (　　　　　), (　　　　　)
4.	金	KIN, KON; (　　　　)	gold, (　　　　　)
5.	土	(　　　), TO;　tsuchi	(　　　　　), soil
6.	川	SEN; (　　　　), [gawa]	(　　　　　　)
7.	中	CHUU; (　　　)	middle, (　　　　), within
8.	山	SAN; (　　　)	(　　　　　)
9.	本	(　　　); moto	book, (　　　　), source
10.	高	KOO; (　　　　)-i	(　　　　　), expensive

B. Match the family name in *kanji* with its *roomaji* equivalent below.

1. 本田 (　　)　　2. 山本 (　　)　　3. 田中 (　　)　　4. 高山 (　　)　　5. 中川 (　　)

a. Nakagawa　　b. Takayama　　c. Yamamoto　　d. Honda　　e. Tanaka

C. Write the appropriate *kanji* for the following words.

1. Friday: _____よう_____　　　　2. Saturday: _____よう_____

D. Fill in the blanks with appropriate words or expressions. Write in *hiragana*.

山中: (making a phone call)

高田: もしもし。

山中: (1) 高田_____ですか。

高田: はい、そうです。

山中: (2) きょうと大学の　山中ですけど、たけしさんは _____か。

高田: 今、るすですけど...。

山中: ああ、そうですか。(3) 何じごろ _____。

高田: 6じごろ かえります。

山中: そうですか。(4) じゃまた _____ でんわします。(5) _____。
　　　　　　　　　　　　　　　　　　(later)　　　　　　　　　　　(Good-bye)

136

E. Read the following excerpt from Mayumi's letter and answer the questions in English.

もうすぐ ふゆやすみ ですね。私は きょねん ほっかいどうに 行って、スキーを

しました。とても たのしかったです。ことしは あねと とうきょうに 行きたい

です。ディズニーランドに 行って、ミッキーマウスと しゃしんを とりたいです。

それから、パレードを 見たいです。ちはるさんは ことしの ふゆやすみに 何を

したいですか。

1. What season is it?   _____

2. What did Mayumi do last year?   _____

3. Which city does she want to go to this year? _____

4. What does she want to do there? (Write 2 things.)

    She wants to _____ and _____.

F. Write a similar letter about your holiday plans.

Moo sugu _____ yasumi desu-ne. Watashi-/Boku-wa kyonen _____-ni
                (season)   (place)

itte, _____. _____.
              (activity)   (adjective commenting on the trip or activity)

Kotoshi-wa _____-to _____-ni ikitai desu.
                (person)   (place)

_____.
              (activity you want to do there)

_____ -san/-kun-wa kotoshi-no _____ yasumi-ni nani-o shitai desu-ka?
  (letter recipient's name)   (season)

G. Now write it in *hiragana* and *kanji*. Write in *katakana* where appropriate.

_____

_____

_____

_____

_____

_____

_____

A. Fill in the chart by writing appropriate answers in *roomaji* and English in the parentheses.

	Kanji	Reading		Meaning	
1.	見	(	)-ru	(	), look at, watch
2.	行	(	)-ku	(	)
3.	来	(	); ( )-ru	(	)
4.	年	(	); toshi	(	)

B. Write the following *kanji* in Arabic numbers.

1. 四 (　　　)   3. 九 (　　　)   5. 二十三 (　　　　)

2. 六 (　　　)   4. 八 (　　　)   6. 五十七 (　　　　)

C. Write the appropriate *kanji* for 1 and 2, and write the reading in *hiragana* for 3 and 4.

1. to watch: ＿＿＿ る   3. 今年: ＿＿ ＿＿ ＿＿

2. to go: ＿＿＿ く   4. 来しゅう: ＿＿ ＿＿ しゅう

D. Fill in the blanks using the cues on the left. Write in *hiragana* and *kanji*. Write the corresponding *katakana* above the *roomaji*.

1. went to

＿＿＿＿＿＿＿＿＿＿ パーティー に ＿＿＿＿＿＿＿＿＿＿。
ka　ra　o　ke

2. saw Dracula

＿＿＿＿＿＿＿＿＿＿＿＿＿＿＿ パーティーで
Ha　ro　wi　i　n

＿＿＿＿＿＿＿＿＿＿＿ を ＿＿＿＿＿＿＿＿＿＿＿＿。
Do　ra　kyu　ra

3. made

＿＿＿＿＿＿＿＿＿＿＿＿＿＿＿ ＿＿＿＿＿＿＿＿＿ を
ba　a　su　de　e　　　　　ke　e　ki

＿＿＿＿＿＿＿＿＿＿＿＿＿＿＿＿＿＿＿＿＿＿＿＿＿。

138

E. Read the following invitation and answer the questions in English.

> 今しゅうの 土よう日は さちこさんの 十八さいの たんじょう日 です。
>
> 金よう日の よる 七じから 私の うちで パーティーを します。みなさん、
>
> ともだちと いっしょに 来てください。たべものは サンドイッチと パスタ
>
> サラダを つくります。みなさんは すきな のみものを もってきて ください。
> bring

1. Whose birthday is coming soon?   _____

2. When is it?   _____

3. What day is the party?   _____

4. What time does it begin?   _____

5. What will be prepared by the host?   _____

6. What are people requested to bring?   _____

F. Write a similar invitation for your own party.

_____-wa _____ desu.
(specific day)   (special occasion)

_____-kara _____-de paatii-o shimasu.
(specific time)   (place)

Mina-san, tomodachi-to issho-ni kite kudasai. Tabemono-wa _____-to
                                                                                          (food item)

_____-o tsukurimasu. Mina-san-wa suki-na nomimono-o motte kite
(food item)

kudasai.

G. Now write it in *hiragana* and *kanji*. Write in *katakana* where appropriate.

_____

_____

_____

_____

_____

_____

A. Fill in the chart by writing appropriate answers in *roomaji* and English in the parentheses.

	Kanji	Reading	Meaning
1.	来	( ); ( )-ru	come
2.	私	( )	( ), privacy
3.	天	( )	sky, ( )
4.	見	( )-ru	see, ( ), watch
5.	水	SUI; ( )	water
6.	年	NEN; ( )	( )

B. Write the appropriate *kanji* for the following words.

1. to watch : _____ る   2. to go: _____ く   3. this week: _____ しゅう

C. What counter words do you use in the following? Write the Arabic number in the parentheses and the counter word in *kanji* (where possible) on the line.

1. 九 _____ : (   ) people   4. 七 _____ : (   ) sheets of paper

2. 八 _____ : (   ) years old   5. 六 _____ : (   ) pens

3. 四年 _____ : for (   ) years

D. Fill in the blanks using the given cues. Write in *hiragana* and *kanji*. Write the corresponding *katakana* above the *roomaji*.

1. 19 members

_____ やきゅうの _____ は 十九 _____
(now)   chi   i   mu
います。

2. watched

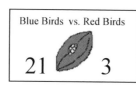

Blue Birds vs. Red Birds

21   3

きのう _____ の _____ を
         fu t to bo o ru   (game)

_____ 。

3. two tickets

ここに _____ の トーナメントの _____ が
            te ni su   chi ke t to

二 _____ あります。だれか _____ ですか。
                                    (want to go)

140

E. Read the following excerpt from Tsuyoshi's letter and answer the questions in English.

ぼくの おとうとは おおさか中学校の サッカーぶに はいっています。

せんしゅうの 土よう日に ぼくは ちちと おおさか中学校と きょうと中学校の

サッカーの しあいに 行きました。天気は とても よかった です。でも しあいは

あまり よくなかった です。おおさか中学校は まけました。スコアは 四たい一

でした。

1. What is the relationship between Tsuyoshi and the soccer player?

　　Tsuyoshi is the _____ of the soccer player.

2. When was the soccer match?　　　　　_____

3. With whom did Tsuyoshi go to the soccer match?　_____

4. How was the weather?　　　　　　_____

5. Which school won the match?　　　_____

6. By how many goals did the winning team win?　_____

F. Write a similar letter about a school sports event you went to.

Watashi/Boku-no_____-wa _____-no
　　　　　　　(friend/family member)　　　　　　　　(school name)

_____-ni haitte-imasu. Senshuu-no_____-ni watashi/boku-wa
　(sports club/team)　　　　　　　　　　　　(day of the week)

_____-to _____-to _____
(friend's name or family member)　(friend/family member's school name)　(another school's name)

-no shiai-ni ikimashita. Tenki-wa _____. Shiai-wa
　　　　　　　　　　　　　　　　(adjective)

_____. _____-wa _____.
　　(adjective)　　　(friend/family member's school name)　　(won/lost)

Sukoa-wa _____ tai _____ deshita.
　　　　　(score)　　　(score)

G. Now write it in *hiragana* and *kanji*. Write in *katakana* where appropriate.

_____

_____

_____

_____

_____

_____

A. Fill in the chart by writing appropriate answers in *roomaji* and English in the parentheses.

	Kanji	Reading	Meaning
1.	学	(　　　　　); mana-bu	(　　　　　); science
2.	校	(　　　　)	(　　　　)
3.	中	CHUU; (　　　　)	(　　　　), inside, within
4.	高	KOO; (　　　　)-i	high, (　　　　)
5.	年	(　　　　); toshi	(　　　　)
6.	上	(　　　　)	(　　　　), up, above, over
7.	下	(　　　　)	(　　　　), down, under

B. Write the appropriate *kanji* for the following words.

1. middle school: ___ ___ ___

2. high school student: ___ ___ せい

3. four years ago: 四 ___ まえ

C. Write the *kanji* for the size of the T-shirts below: 大 、中、小.

 (　　　)　　　 (　　　)　　　 (　　　)

D. Fill in the blanks using the given cues. Write in *hiragana* and *kanji*. Write in *katakana* where appropriate. Write the prices in Arabic numbers.

1.

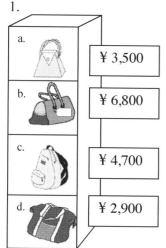

a. ￥ 3,500

b. ￥ 6,800

c. ￥ 4,700

d. ￥ 2,900

Q. 上から 二ばんめの かばんは いくらですか。

A. _____ です。

Q. いちばん下のは いくらですか。

A. _____ です。

A._____が _____か。
(What do you need?)

B. _____ と _____が

_____。

2. Shopping
List
tomatoes
milk

E. Read the following passage and answer the questions in English.

今、日本は ふゆものの バーゲンセールの きせつ です。今日、あねと デパートで
　　　　　　winter clothes
かいものを しました。きいろい くつを かいました。それから セーターを 五まい

かいました。やすかったから、たくさん かいました。あねは ジーンズを 二本

かいました。かいものは とても たのしかったです。

1. When did the author shop? _____

2. Where did she go shopping? _____

3. What did she buy besides shoes? How many did she buy? _____

4. Why did she buy so many? _____

5. What did her sister buy? How many did she buy? _____

F. Write a similar passage about yourself.

Watashi/Boku-wa _____ -to _____ -de
　　　　　　　　　　　　(a person)　　　　　　　　　　　　　(name of the store)

_____. _____ -o
　　　　　　(shopped)　　　　　　　　　　　　(name of one item that you bought)

_____ -to _____ -o _____
(number + counter)　　(name of the other item that you bought)　　(number + counter)

kaimashita. _____ -kara kaimashita.
　　　　　　　　(reason for buying these items)

G. Now write it in *hiragana* and *kanji*. Write in *katakana* where appropriate.

_____

_____

_____

_____

_____

_____

A. Fill in the chart by writing appropriate answers in *roomaji* and English in the parentheses.

	Kanji	Reading	Meaning
1.	円	( )	( ), circle
2.	百	( ) [BYAKU, PYAKU]	( )
3.	千	( ) [ZEN]	( )
4.	高	( ); taka-i	expensive, ( )
5.	見	( )-ru	see, ( ), watch
6.	金	KIN; ( )	gold, ( )

B. Read the following price tags written in *kanji* and write the price in Arabic numbers below.

1. 七千二百円 (   )

2. 四千三百円 (   )

3. 六千百五十円 (   )

C. Write the appropriate readings of these *kanji* in *roomaji*.

1. 八百 (   )   3. 三千 (   )

2. 九百 (   )   4. 八千 (   )

D. Fill in the blanks using the given cues. Write in *hiragana* and *kanji*. Write the corresponding *katakana* above the *roomaji*.

1.

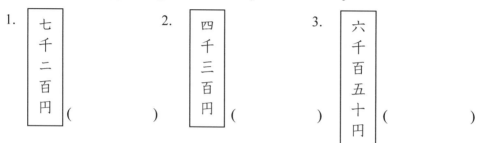

A: _____に _____を
   Ba   re   n   ta   i   n   (what)

_____か。
                (did you receive?)

B: _____を _____。
   cho ko re e to   (received)

2.

floor: items
5F Books
4F Music, Videos
3F Clothes
2F Electronics
1F Bags, Accessories

A: _____。
              (Excuse me.)

DVDは _____か。
              (which floor)

B: 四かいです。

144

E. Read the following passage and answer the questions in English.

私は よく デパートに 行きます。 たくさん おいしい たべものが ある から、 ちか が 一ばん すき です。 ちかで よく イタリアンジェラートを たべます。 七かいも すき です。 七かいに ゆうびんきょくと 本やが あります。 その 本やで ときどき ざっしを かいます。 日本の デパートに 行った ことが ありますか。

1. What is this passage mainly about?　　　_____

2. Which floor is the writer's most favorite?　_____

3. What does he do there?　　　　　　　　_____

4. What other floor does he mention in this passage?　_____

5. What do you find on this floor?　　　　　_____

F. Write a similar passage about your favorite section of a department store or shopping mall.

Watashi/Boku-no machi-ni _____-ga arimasu.
　　　　　　　　　　　　　　　(name of a department store / mall)

_____-ni takusan omise-ga arimasu.
　　　　(name of a department store / mall)

Watashi/Boku-wa _____-ga _____desu.
　　　　　　　　　　(name of the store)　　　　　　(like the best)

_____-wa _____-ni arimasu. Soko-de _____-o
　(name of the store)　　　　　(floor level)　　　　　　　　　　(name of the item)

kaimasu. Watashi/Boku-wa _____-mo suki desu. _____
　　　　　　　　　　(name of another store)　　　　　　　　(name of another store)

-wa _____-ni arimasu. _____
　　(floor level)　　　　　　　　(Have you ever been to an American department store or mall?)

G. Now write it in *hiragana* and *kanji*. Write in *katakana* where appropriate.

_____

_____

_____

_____

_____

_____

A. Fill in the chart by writing appropriate answers in *roomaji* and English in the parentheses.

	Kanji	Reading	Meaning
1.	口	(　　　　　　) [guchi]	(　　　　　　), opening
2.	目	(　　　　)	(　　　　); *ordinal suffix*
3.	耳	(　　　　)	(　　　　)
4.	天	(　　　　)	(　　　　), heaven
5.	元	(　　　　)	(　　　　), foundation
6.	気	(　　　　)	(　　　　), energy, attention

B. Match the following words with the pictures.

1. 口 (　　)　　　　3. はな (　　)　　　　5. 耳 (　　)　　　　7. 目 (　　)

2. て (　　)　　　　4. あし (　　)　　　　6. は (　　)

a)　　　　b)　　　　c)　　　　d)　　　　e)　　　　f)　　　　g)

C. Change the given sentences to sentences in the past tense as if you were writing about what happened to you. Write in *hiragana*.

	present "*n desu*"	present tense	past tense
Ex. 1	おなかが いたいんです。	おなかが いたいです。	おなかが いたかったです。
Ex. 2	かぜなんです。	かぜです。	かぜでした。
1.	あたまが いたいんです。	あたまが いたいです。	あたまが ＿＿＿＿＿＿＿＿＿＿＿＿。
2.	ねつが あるんです。	ねつが あります。	ねつが ＿＿＿＿＿＿＿＿＿＿＿＿。

D. Complete the following dialogue using the cues on the left. Write in *hiragana*.

after meals

A: いつ この ＿＿＿＿＿＿＿＿＿＿＿＿＿を のみますか。

B: ＿＿＿＿＿＿＿＿＿＿＿ の ＿＿＿＿＿＿＿＿＿＿＿＿＿

＿＿＿＿＿＿＿＿＿＿＿＿＿ ください。

E. Read the following excerpt from a letter and answer the questions in English.

お元気ですか。ボストンの 今日の 天気は はれですけど、かぜが つよい
です。私は せんしゅう かぜ でした。土よう日は 一日中 ねていました。
ねつが ありました。それから、のどが いたかったです。みゆきさんは
大じょうぶですか。さむい です から、からだに 気をつけてくださいね。

1. Describe today's weather in Boston.　　_____

2. What happened to the writer last week?　_____

3. On which day did she sleep all day long?　_____

4. What were her symptoms?　　　　　　_____

5. What did she ask Miyuki?　　　　　　_____

F. Imagine that you were sick last week, and write a similar letter sharing your experience.

O-genki desu-ka? _____ -no kyoo-no tenki-wa _____
　　　　　　　　　　(name of your town)　　　　　　　　　　　　(description of weather)

desu. _____.
　　　　(additional information about the weather: temperature, wind, etc.)

Watashi/Boku-wa senshuu byooki deshita. _____
　　　　　　　　　　　　　　　　　　　　　　　(symptoms of the illness)

_____.

_____ -san/kun-wa daijoobu desu-ka? Karada-ni ki-o tsukete kudasai-ne.
　　(pen pal's name)

G. Now write it in *hiragana* and *kanji*. Write in *katakana* where appropriate.

_____

_____

_____

_____

_____

_____

_____

147

A. Fill in the chart by writing appropriate answers in *roomaji* and English in the parentheses.

	Kanji	Reading	Meaning
1.	名	( )	( )
2.	前	( )	( ), front
3.	オ	( )	talent; *suffix for counting* ( )
4.	高	KOO; ( )-i	( ), expensive
5.	金	( ); kane	gold; ( )
6.	気	( )	spirit, ( ), attention

B. Write the appropriate *kanji* for 1 through 3, and write the English meaning for 4 and 5.

1. one year old: 一 ____   3. blond: ___ぱつ   5. 名前: _____

2. tall: せが___い   4. 気がみじかい: _____

C. Complete the answers to the question below using the cues on the left. Write in *hiragana* and *kanji*.

Q. どんな人ですか。

1. kind and cheerful

_____ て _____ 人です。

2. quiet and serious

_____ で _____ 人です。

3. short with brown hair

_____ が _____ 、

_____ が _____ 人です。

4. tall with short hair

_____ が _____ 、

_____ が _____ 人です。

D. Read the following passage and answer the questions in English.

この人の 名前は 山田けんじ さん です。けんじさんは 二十一
才 です。けんじさんは せが 高くて、かみが くろくて みじかい
です。元気で おもしろい人 です。きょ年、私の たんじょうび
パーティーで けんじさんに あいました。

1. What is this person's name?　　_____

2. How old is he?　　_____

3. Describe his physical features.　　_____

4. Describe his personality.　　_____

5. Where did this author meet him?　　_____

E. Write a similar passage to describe someone you know.

Kono hito-no namae-wa _____ desu. _____-san/kun-wa
　　　　　　　　　　　　　　　(name of the person)　　　　　　　　(name of the person)

_____ desu. _____ -san/kun-wa se-ga _____,
(age of the person)　　　(name of the person)　　　　　　　　　(height: tall or short)

kami-ga _____ _____ desu.
　　　　　(color of the hair)　　　　　　(hair: long or short)

_____ hito desu.
(description of his/her personality: Use two adjectives.)

_____ -de _____ -san/kun-ni aimashita.
(place/event where you met this person)　　(name of the person)

F. Now write it in *hiragana* and *kanji*. Write in *katakana* where appropriate.

_____

_____

_____

_____

_____

_____

A. Fill in the chart by writing appropriate answers in *roomaji* and English in the parentheses.

	Kanji	Reading	Meaning
1.	才	( )	talent; *suffix for counting* ( )
2.	先	( )	( ), ahead
3.	生	( ); ( )-mareru	birth, ( ), be born
4.	母	( ), o-( )-san	( )
5.	父	( ), o-( )-san	( )
6.	子	( ) [go]	( )

B. Write the readings in *hiragana* for 1 and 2, and write appropriate *kanji* for 3 and 4.

1. 父と母: ___ ___ と ___ ___   3. 18 yrs. old: 十八 _____

2. 子どもの 名前: ___どもの ___ ___ ___   4. teacher: ___ ___

C. Fill in the blanks using the cues on the left to complete sentences about Tim-*sensei*. Write in *hiragana* and *kanji*. Write the corresponding *katakana* above the *roomaji*.

1. born in Michigan, Nov. 21

ティム _____ は 11 _____ 21 _____ に _____
　　　　　　　　　　　　　　　　　　　　　　　　　　　Mi shi ga n

で _____ まれました。

2. lived in

_____ DC に 十二年かん _____
Wa shi n to n

3. taught English
    in

_____ で 二年かん _____ を _____

4.

1989年に _____ で _____
　　　　　　　Ha wa i

in Hawaii

D. Read the following passage and answer the questions in English.

　テーラーさんは 二十九オの カナダ人です。 せが 高くて、 あかるい人です。
テーラーさんは バンクーバーで 生まれました。 子どものとき、 とうきょうに
すんでいました。 今は シアトルに 一人で すんでいます。 けっこん していません
けど、 来年の 五月に 日本人の おんなの人と けっこんします。

1. How old is Mr. Taylor? _____

2. What is his nationality? _____

3. Describe him. (physical appearance and personality) _____

4. Where was he born? _____

5. Where did he live when he was a child? _____

6. Where does he live now? _____

7. When is he getting married? _____

8. Who is he getting married to? _____

E. Write a similar passage about a real or imaginary person.

_____-san-wa _____-sai-no _____-jin desu. _____
　　(person's name)　　　　　(age)　　　　(nationality)　　　　　　　(physical description)

_____ hito desu. _____-san-wa _____-de umaremashita.
(personality description)　　　　　(person's name)　　　　(place of birth)

Kodomo-no-toki _____-ni sunde-imashita. Ima-wa _____
　　　　　(place s/he lived as a child)　　　　　　　　　　(place s/he lives now)

-ni sunde-imasu. _____. _____
　　　　　　(whether s/he is married or not)　　　　　(when s/he will marry/got married)

-ni _____.
　　(will marry/got married)

F. Now write it in *hiragana* and *kanji*. Write in *katakana* where appropriate.

_____

_____

_____

_____

_____

_____

A. Fill in the chart by writing appropriate answers in *roomaji* and English in the parentheses.

	Kanji	Reading	Meaning
1.	言	(　　　)-u	(　　　　　　　)
2.	話	(　　　)-su	(　　　　　　　)
3.	読	(　　　)-mu	(　　　　　　　)
4.	国	KOKU [GOKU]; (　　　　　)	(　　　　　　　)
5.	語	(　　　　　　　)	(　　　　　), speech
6.	子	(　　　　　) [go]	(　　　　　　　)

B. Choose the direct object that the following verbs take and write its letter in the parentheses.

1. 読む (　　) 　　　2. 話す (　　) 　　　3. きく (　　) 　　　4. 見る (　　)

a. しんぶん 　　　b. おんがく 　　　c. えいが 　　　d. 中国語

C. Answer the question below using the cues on the left. Write in *hiragana* and *kanji*. Write the corresponding *katakana* above the *roomaji*.

Q: しょうらい、何をしたいですか。

1. become a teacher

A: ＿＿＿＿＿＿＿＿の ＿＿＿＿＿＿に ＿＿＿＿＿＿＿です
　　　pi　a　no

2. live in

A: ＿＿＿＿＿＿に ＿＿＿＿＿＿＿＿＿です。
　　I　ta　ri　a

3. work at a big

bank
$

A: ＿＿＿＿＿＿ ＿＿＿＿＿で ＿＿＿＿＿＿＿です。

4.

A: ＿＿＿＿＿＿＿＿＿＿＿＿＿＿＿＿＿です。

152

D. Read the following excerpt from a letter and answer the questions in English.

私は 今 大学生です。二年ごに そつぎょうします。そのあと、パリとニースに りょこうします。しょうらい、小学校の フランス語の 先生に なりたいです。 そして、けっこんしたいです。子どもが 二人 ほしいです。

1. When will the writer graduate? _____

2. What will she do after graduation? _____

3. What does she want to do in the future? _____

4. What about marriage? _____

5. How many children does she want? _____

E. Write a similar passage about yourself.

Watashi/Boku-wa _____ desu. _____ sotsugyoo shimasu.
　　　　　　　　　　(grade)　　　　　　　　　　(when you will graduate)

Sono ato, _____.
　　　　　　　(what you will do after you graduate)

Shoorai, _____.
　　　　　(what you want to do/be in the future)

Soshite, kekkon _____ desu. Kodomo-ga _____ hoshii desu.
　　　　　　　(whether you want to marry or not)　　　　　(number)
/Kodomo-wa hoshiku-nai desu.

F. Now write it in *hiragana* and *kanji*. Write in *katakana* where appropriate.

_____

_____

_____

_____

_____

_____

A. Fill in the chart by writing appropriate answers in *roomaji* and English in the parentheses.

	Kanji	Reading	Meaning
1.	書	(　　　)-ku	(　　　　　　)
2.	聞	(　　　)-ku	(　　　　　　), listen to, ask
3.	間	(　　　　　)	space, (　　　　　　　)
4.	時	(　　　　); toki [doki]	(　　　　), *counter for clock hours*
5.	分	(　　　) [PUN]; wa-karu	(　　　), *counter for minutes*; understand
6.	雨	(　　　　)	(　　　　　)
7.	雪	(　　　　)	(　　　　　)

B. Read the following phrases and choose the appropriate situation when you would most likely use the phrase. Write the letter in the parentheses.

1. すみません、かんじで 書いて ください。（　　　　）

2. 分かりません。先生に 聞いて ください。　（　　　　）

a. You can't read the Chinese characters written on the Japanese menu.
b. You want to know how your Japanese friend's name is written in Chinese characters.
c. Your classmate asks you how to say a word in Japanese, but you have not learned the word yet.

C. Complete the answers below using the cues on the left. Write in *hiragana* and *kanji*.

1. 12 days

Q: りょこうは 何日間ですか。

A: ＿＿＿＿＿＿＿＿＿＿＿＿＿ です。

2. 1 hr. and 45 mins.
　 by *shinkansen*

Q: とうきょうから きょうとまで 何時間ですか。

A: ＿＿＿＿＿＿＿＿＿＿＿＿＿＿＿＿＿＿＿ です

3. at 12:07 p.m.

Itinerary to Rome

leave　6/21 at 3:00 p.m.
arrive　6/22 at 12:07 p.m.

Q: いつ ローマに つきますか。

A: ＿＿＿＿＿＿＿＿＿＿＿＿＿＿＿＿＿ つきます。

D. Read the following postcard and answer the questions in English.

お元気ですか。今、ふゆやすみで 日本に 来ました。お天気は あまり よくない です。まい日、雨です。今日は 雪で、とても さむいです。きのう、かまくらの <u>大ぶつ</u>を 見ました。その 大ぶつは 七百五十年の れきしが あります。今日から
big Buddha

きょうとに 六日間 行きます。金かくじと りょうあんじに 行きたいです。 りょうあんじは ゆうめいな ぜんの <u>おてら</u>です。十二月三十日に アメリカに
temple

かえります。よい お年を。

1. Which vacation is the writer on? _____
2. What country is he in? _____
3. Describe today's weather. _____
4. What is the temperature today? _____
5. How old is the Big Buddha of Kamakura? _____
6. How many days will he stay in Kyoto? _____

E. Imagine that you are traveling. Write a postcard to your Japanese teacher or friend.

_____. Ima, _____-de, _____-ni
(opening greeting)　　　　　　　(name of the holiday or vacation)　　　　(name of the place)

kimashita. O-tenki-wa _____-de, _____ desu.
　　　　　　　　　　　　(weather)　　　　　　　(comment on the temperature)

_____ _____.
(time word)　　　　　　　　　(activity that you did)

_____-wa _____.
(the activity/object)　　　　　(description of the activity/object. Use adjective(s).)

_____-kara _____-ni ikimasu.
(time word)　　　　　　　　　　　(name of the place)

_____-de _____.
(place)　　　　　　　　　　　(activity that you want to do. Use the -tai form.)

_____-ni _____-ni kaerimasu.
(time word)　　　　　　　　　　　(name of the place)

_____.
(closing greeting)

F. Now write it in *hiragana* and *kanji*. Write in *katakana* where appropriate.

_____
_____
_____
_____
_____
_____
_____

A. Fill in the chart by writing appropriate answers in *roomaji* and English in the parentheses.

	Kanji	Reading	Meaning
1.	東	( ), higashi	( )
2.	京	( ), KEI	( )
3.	駅	( )	( )
4.	百	( ) [BYAKU, PYAKU]	( )
5.	千	( ) [ZEN]	( )

B. Write the following in Arabic numbers. Then match the number with one of the facts listed below, and write its letter in the parentheses.

1. 七百八十三万   2. 千八百六十三   3. 八百五十

_____ (   )   _____ (   )   _____ (   )

   a. This is the year Tokyo became capital of Japan.
   b. This is the number (in feet) of Tokyo Tower's highest observation point.
   c. This is the approximate population of Tokyo.

C. Read the sentences below and in Japanese write the names of the buildings described on the line. (If you need help, re-read the textbook, Culture Notes in Lesson 59.)

1. 日本で 一ばん 高い ビル です。 しんじゅくに あります。

_____

2. 今は てんのうが すんでいます。 そのまえは しょうぐんが すんでいました。
    Emperor

_____

3. めいじてんのうの じんじゃ です。 大きい こうえんが あります。

_____

Imperial Palace (*Kookyo*)
National Parliament Building (*Kokkai-gijidoo*)
Meiji-jinguu Shrine (*Meiji Jinguu*)
Tokyo Tower (*Tookyoo Tawaa*)
Tokyo City Hall (*Tochoo*)

D. Read the following passage and answer the questions in English.

あした、でんしゃで 東京駅に つきます。そのあと、<u>六本木</u>ヒルズで
（ろっぽんぎ）
a district in Tokyo

かいものをします。六本木ヒルズに たくさんあたらしい おみせが あります。

ブーツが ほしいです。それから、<u>いけぶくろ</u>の サンシャインビルに 行きたい
a district in Tokyo

です。ビルは 六十かい あります。 十かいの <u>すいぞくかん</u>に 行きたいです。
aquarium

よる、六十かいから 東京の まちを 見たいです。 東京は 大きくてきれい

<u>でしょうね</u>。
adjective + *deshoo* is used when you imagine how something/someone looks or is.

1. Where will this writer arrive by train?　　　_____

2. What will she do next?　　　　　　　　　_____

3. What does she want in Roppongi?　　　　　_____

4. How many floors does the Sunshine Building have?　_____

5. On which floor can you find the aquarium?　_____

E. Research Tokyo's sight-seeing spots. Then write a brief passage about your plans in Tokyo.

_____ (-ni) _____-de, _____-ni
　　　(time word)　　　　　　　　　　(means of transportation)　　　　　(a place)

tsukimasu. Sono ato, _____-de _____.
　　　　　　　　　　　(another place)　　　　　　　　　(activity that you will do)

_____-wa _____.
　　　(the place)　　　　　　　　　(description of the place)

_____-de _____.
　　　(another place)　　　　　　　(activity that you want to do: Use –*tai* form.)

Sorekara, _____-ni _____.
　　　　　　　(another place)　　　　　　　(want to go: Use -*tai* form.)

F. Now write it in *hiragana* and *kanji*. Write in *katakana* where appropriate.

_____

_____

_____

_____

_____

_____

Made in the USA
Middletown, DE
30 December 2020